HOW TO THRIVE AFTER 55

Unlock Ageless Vitality with 7 Proven Habits for Energy and Longevity

LIZA LLUMA

LLUMA BOOKS

Hear the book come alive!

Scan for a unique discussion of key insights by AI-hosts Mac and Molly.

www.lizalluma.com/after55/#thrive55-deep-dive

DISCLAIMER

This book is based on research and contains the opinions and ideas of its author. It is intended to provide helpful and informative material on the subjects addressed in the publication. It is sold with the understanding that the author and publisher are not engaged in rendering medical, health, or other professional advice to the individual reader. The reader should not use the information contained in this book as a substitute for the advice of a licensed health care professional. To the best of the author's knowledge, the information provided is accurate at the time of its publication. The author disclaims any liability whatsoever with respect to any loss, injury, or damage arising directly or indirectly from the use of this book.

Contents

Preface

Is it luck, or do our lifestyle choices determine how well we age?

Since my early years, digestive troubles and a curiosity about my own body nudged me towards a healthier lifestyle. Facing aging and illness is tough, but I've empowered myself by putting into practice what I've learned. Since turning fifty, I've been striving to stay vibrant, convincing myself that I've still got it! I've been eating better, exercising more, and enjoying the outdoors, though it's hard to keep up the pace sometimes. This personal journey led me to write this guidebook.

Together with my father and brother, we spent over a year learning about healthy living. We sifted through our research to highlight the most essential and manageable strategies for good health and well-being, making it easier for you to apply them. As a result, we put all these refined insights and stories into this book.

In my forties, after relocating from Australia to Catalonia, Spain, I embraced the Mediterranean diet, hiking, and gardening. However, in my fifties, during what I call my 'mid-century modern life crisis,' I noticed hormonal changes: sleep issues, weight gain, mood swings, indigestion, and painful joints. I felt more tired, my skin started sagging, and my muscles diminished. A friend joked it was like going from a cherry to a prune. But I'm determined to stay a plum as long as I can.

On the other hand, my brother hasn't been as fortunate. Chronic illnesses and severe diseases hit him hard as he entered his fifties. Despite this, he keeps his sense of humor, proving laughter is truly the best medicine.

My parents, now in their eighties, often laugh when I suggest ways to stay healthy. They prefer to relax and indulge occasionally, yet they go to the gym, do water aerobics, enjoy time with friends, eat well, and opt for low-alcohol wine. My father struggles with sleep, and my mother has polymyalgia rheumatica, a muscle condition common after fifty. Despite these challenges, they cherish their joyful lives and joke that the best part of getting old is that it doesn't last long.

Even with a family history of cancer, diabetes, and heart issues, I believe lifestyle choices are crucial for our healthspan. Perhaps that's why you picked up this book. Considering your own family history, are you inspired to make healthy decisions to live a vibrant life for as long as possible?

Crafted for those who've gathered a few more candles on the cake, *How To Thrive After 55* dives into the seven key lifestyle habits that will keep a spring in your step: quality sleep, regular exercise, balanced nutrition, mindful alcohol consumption, robust physical health, mental well-being, and nurturing friendships.

I hope this guidebook helps you improve your health habits. Get ready for better days, embrace humor, and take control of your health. Every small effort counts.

Liza Lluma

"THEY SAY AGE IS ALL IN YOUR MIND. GOOD THING I FORGET HOW OLD I AM HALF THE TIME!"

Introduction

Ready to Transform Your Life?

As you age, change can become increasingly challenging. You may find comfort in your routines, and breaking away from them can seem like climbing a mountain. But guess what? You've already laced up your boots and taken that initial step—by getting this workbook. Now, the question remains—will this book join the dusty ranks of untouched self-help manuals, or will it become a crucial companion on your journey to a healthier you? The choice lies in your hands—or feet, so to speak.

Why This Book is Your Ally

The true secret is not about grand, sweeping changes, but about small, consistent modifications in your daily routine—habits that are workable and sustainable. Let's be candid; adulthood often brings a certain rigidity. You give yourself a few chances to succeed before you retreat into your old ways. But here's where this workbook comes in—it's your reliable comrade accompanying you on this transformative journey. This guide equips you with useful tools and offers a straightforward method for documenting your growth and outcomes.

It's Your Turn... (Are You up for It?)

When you reach the end of this book, you will receive not just a comprehensive picture of your progress, but also a clear pathway to maintaining your well-being. This is not about becoming an overnight sensation, but about adopting a gradual approach towards better health. Are you ready to take charge on this path towards well-being? This is your opportunity to form habits that will persist, weaving into your daily routine.

Just remember, this isn't a sprint—it's a marathon; we are not hares, but tortoises. Get ready to step up, embrace a healthier lifestyle, and bask in the happiness that comes with it, especially in your golden years. Every epic journey begins with a single stride. Are you willing to take yours?

Mastering QR codes

Throughout this book you will find QR codes that link to either downloadable PDFs or more information about the topic.

1. Scan QR code with your smartphone

Point your smartphone's camera at the QR code printed in the book until the prompt appears to access the webpage.

If your phone doesn't have the built-in QR code reader in your camera app, you'll need to download and install one from your phone's app store.

2. Printable log sheets

If the QR code leads to a printable PDF, the app may prompt you to download or open the PDF. Follow the on-screen instructions to do so.

The PDF file is downloaded to your phone's downloads folder, which you can then email to yourself and print out from your computer.

3. Website links

If the QR code leads to more information about a topic, tapping on the link should open the website in your phone's browser.
From there, you can read the additional information provided.

The 7 Key Lifestyle Habits Unveiled

This book focuses on the seven essential habits needed for a healthy and satisfying life. While every section matters, prioritize the ones that are most significant to your personal goals and values.

1. **SLEEP: More Than Just a Necessity**
   Enough quality sleep in the correct environment

2. **EXERCISE: Small Steps, Big Gains**
   Physical activity suited to your needs

3. **NUTRITION: Savor Every Bite**
   Eating a balanced diet & adequate hydration

4. **ALCOHOL: A Healthier Sip Strategy**
   Low-risk drinking or not at all

5. **PHYSICAL HEALTH: Every Move Counts**
   Preventing & managing health conditions

6. **MENTAL WELL-BEING: Daily Harmony**
   Coping effectively with life's challenges

7. **FRIENDSHIPS: The Joy Prescription**
   Feeling connected & supported

Quick Start Guide

Welcome to your personal health guide! Instead of sweaty high-fives, this book offers practical steps. It begins by evaluating your current health. Then, it delves into the seven lifestyle habits where you'll learn the basics, make an action plan, track your habits using log pages, and journal your progress. It wraps up with a review of your health and happiness, offering guidance for ongoing improvement.

1 Initial Self-Assessment

Start with quick journal questions to assess your current state across the seven lifestyle habits covered in this book.

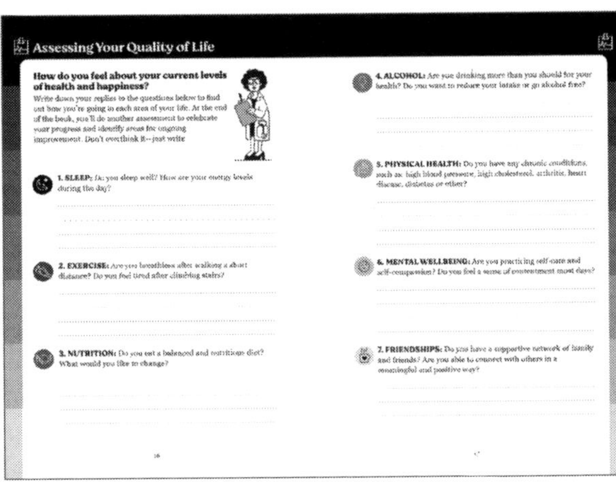

Assessing Your Quality of Life

How do you feel about your current levels of health and happiness?

Write down your replies to the questions below to find out how you're going in each area of your life. At the end of the book, you'll do another assessment to celebrate your progress and identify areas for ongoing improvement. Don't overthink it—just write

1. SLEEP: Do you sleep well? How are your energy levels during the day?

2. EXERCISE: Are you breathless after walking a short distance? Do you feel tired after climbing stairs?

3. NUTRITION: Do you eat a balanced and nutritious diet? What would you like to change?

4. ALCOHOL: Are you drinking more than you should for your health? Do you want to reduce your intake or go alcohol free?

5. PHYSICAL HEALTH: Do you have any chronic conditions, such as high blood pressure, high cholesterol, arthritis, heart disease, diabetes or other?

6. MENTAL WELLBEING: Are you practicing self-care and self-compassion? Do you feel a sense of contentment most days?

7. FRIENDSHIPS: Do you have a supportive network of family and friends? Are you able to connect with others in a meaningful and positive way?

2 Wellness Wheel

The Wellness Wheel visually shows your current status and satisfaction levels at a glance.

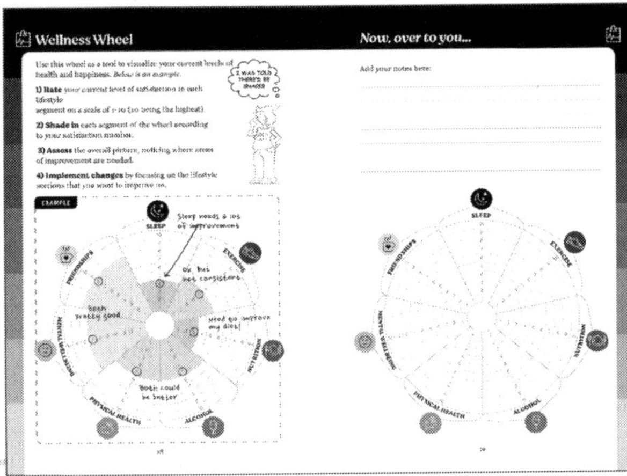

Wellness Wheel

Use this wheel as a tool to visualize your current levels of health and happiness. *Below is an example.*

1) Rate your current level of satisfaction in each lifestyle segment on a scale of 1-10 (10 being the highest).

2) Shade in each segment of the wheel according to your satisfaction number.

3) Assess the overall picture, noticing where areas of improvement are needed.

4) Implement changes by focusing on the lifestyle sections that you want to improve on.

Now, over to you...

Add your notes here:

3 Learn the Basics

Discover essential tips and guidelines for each lifestyle area to establish a solid foundation. Decide whether to concentrate on all areas or just the ones most important to your needs.

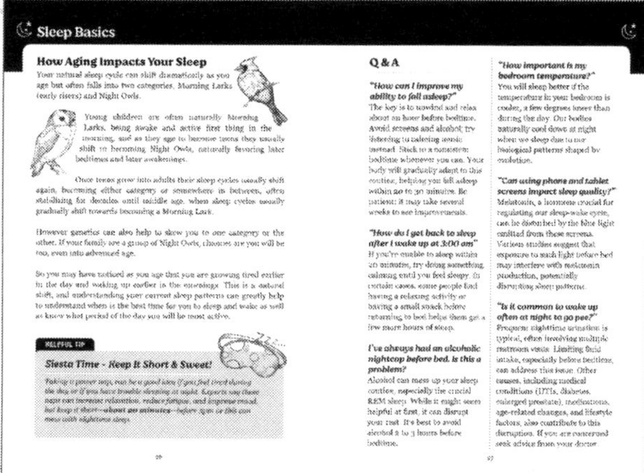

4 Formulate an Action Plan

An action plan provides specific steps and goals to help you stick to your new habits.

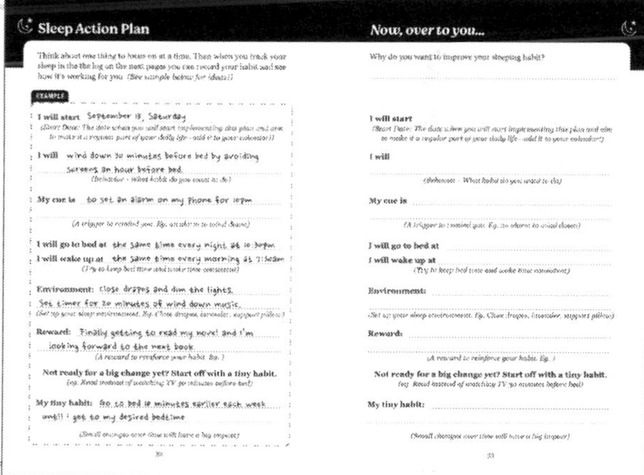

5 Log Your Progress

Use the log pages to keep track of your lifestyle habits.

6 Reflect on Your Progress

Use journal pages to celebrate your successes and pinpoint areas to improve.

Sleep Journal

What changes would you make to your sleeping place to make it more sleep-friendly?

What are some stressors in your life, and how can you manage or minimize them?

Are there relaxation techniques that resonate with you and that you would like to incorporate?

Have you tried getting some sunlight exposure in the mornings? If yes, what benefits have you felt? If not, what could be some ways to do so?

Celebrating Successes

What are some positive changes you've noticed in your sleep patterns since starting this journal? How have these changes impacted your daily life?

Lessons from Setbacks

What are some common factors that seem to disrupt your sleep? How can you make adjustments to address these factors and improve your sleep quality?

7 Analyze

Review how small changes affect your lifestyle. Note down health appointments and discussions with your healthcare professional.

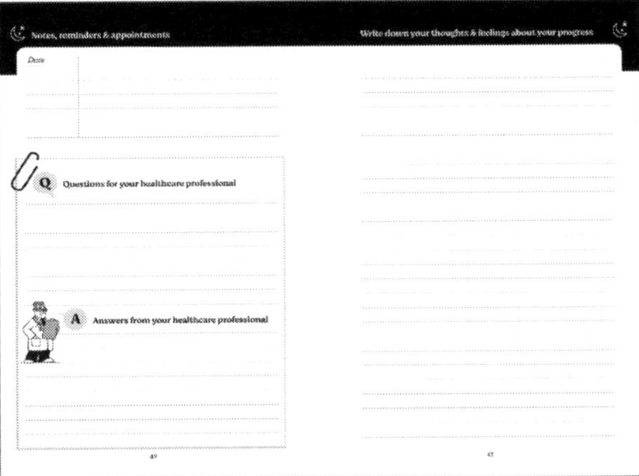
Notes, reminders & appointments

Write down your thoughts & feelings about your progress

Date

Q Questions for your healthcare professional

A Answers from your healthcare professional

8 Rinse & Repeat

Read heartfelt stories about others' personal challenges.

Scan the QR code at the end of each section to download and print additional log sheets.

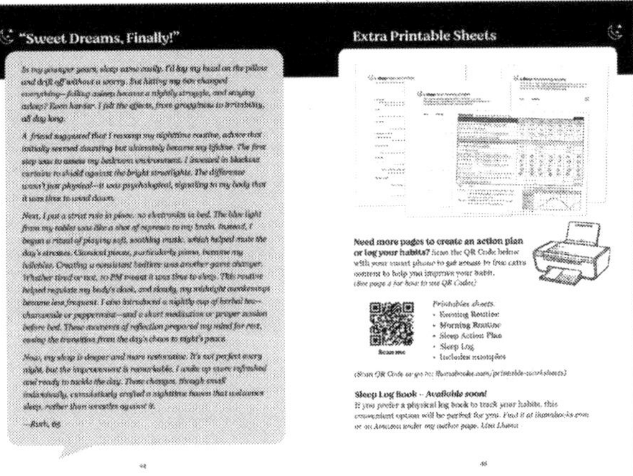
"Sweet Dreams, Finally!"

Extra Printable Sheets

Need more pages to create an action plan or log your habits? Scan the QR Code below with your smart phone to get access to free extra content to help you improve your habit.

Printables sheets:
- Evening Routine
- Morning Routine
- Sleep Action Plan
- Sleep Log

Sleep Log Book – Available soon!

9 Self-Assess Again

Evaluate how the changes you've made have impacted your life and whether they have been beneficial.

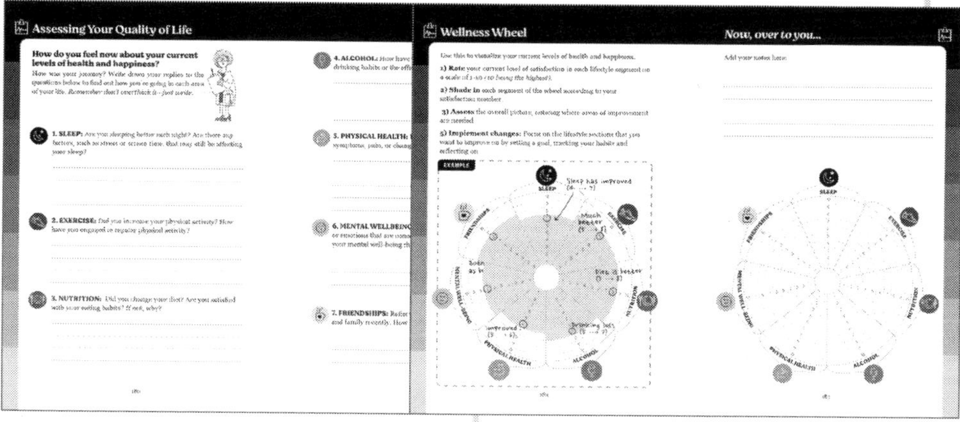

10 Going Forward

Commit to maintaining your positive habits consistently. These pages will support you in living a happier and healthier life, even after you finish this book.

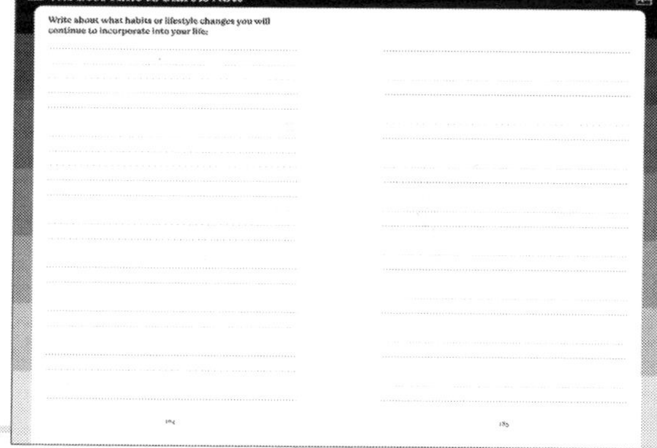

It all takes time!

Success isn't a direct path; it has its ups and downs. Don't dwell on daily fluctuations, but focus on the bigger picture. This guided workbook aims to help you improve your health and happiness step by step, making lasting changes. Every little step counts towards your overall success.

The Power of Tracking Your Progress

Making lasting changes requires time and taking small, achievable steps to alter habits on a manageable scale. That's where the log sheets in this book come in handy. While there are only a few sheets provided, for sustained long-term change, you'll need more.

Here's a couple of ways you can get them:

Scan me

- Follow the QR code link to our website and download the free PDF log sheets, printing out as many as you want.
- Buy the individual log books in this series, which will allow you to track your health habits for longer than a couple of weeks. *Go to: www.lizalluma.com/after55*

Sleep Log Improve your sleep quality by keeping a log. **EXAMPLE**

Fill out in the morning *(within 3 hours of waking up)*	Sun	Mon	Tue	Wed	Thu	Fri	Sat
What time did you turn off the lights to go to sleep last night?	11:30pm	10:45pm	10:30pm	10:30pm	11pm	11:30pm	10:15pm
What time did you wake up today?	7:30am	8:15am	8 am	8 am	8:30am	8:45am	8 am
How many total hours did you sleep *(or try to sleep)* last night?	6hrs	7.5 hrs	9 hrs	8 hrs	7 hrs	6.5 hrs	8 hrs
How many times did you wake up during the night?	5	3	1	1	2	4	2
Yesterday's factors that might have impacted your sleep quality:							
Did you nap yesterday? If yes, what time?	4pm		4:30pm			1:30pm	
• How long did you nap?	20min		10min			30min	
Have caffeine after...3 pm....? *(Write your cut off time. eg. 3pm)* *[coffee, tea, caffeinated soda, chocolate, energy drinks, certain medications]*	Y/(N)	Y/(N)	Y/(N)	Y/(N)	Y/(N)	(Y)/N	Y/(N)
Have alcohol after .....7 pm.....? *(Write your cut off time. eg. 6pm)*	(Y)/N	Y/(N)	Y/(N)	Y/(N)	Y/(N)	Y/(N)	Y/(N)
Have nicotine after ....? *(Write your cut off time. eg. 6pm)*	~~Y/N~~	~~Y/N~~	~~Y/N~~	~~Y/N~~	~~Y/N~~	~~Y/N~~	~~Y/N~~
Did you exercise?	Y/(N)	Y/(N)	(Y)/N	(Y)/N	(Y)/N	Y/(N)	Y/(N)
Eat a heavy meal after .....6 pm.....? *(Write your cut off time. eg. 6pm)*	(Y)/N	Y/(N)	Y/(N)	Y/(N)	(Y)/N	(Y)/N	Y/(N)
Take any sleeping medication? *(Pharmaceutical, Herbal or Botanical)*							Ambien
• What time and amount of medication?							11pm, 5mg

Date	*Notes*
23rd June	I went to bed later than normal and had a really hard time falling asleep. It could have been from the alcohol and heavy meal.
25th June	Amazing night sleep! I think the morning walk helped and I went to bed on time too.

Rate your sleep quality each night to determine any trends

	Sun	Mon	Tue	Wed	Thu	Fri	Sat
Excellent							
Good			•	•			
Average					•		•
Fair		•					
Poor	•					•	

www.llumabooks.com/printable-worksheets

How to create lasting habits in four steps

According to James Clear, the author of "Atomic Habits", there are four simple steps for you to create lasting change in your life through developing small, consistent habits.

1) Make use of "tiny habits"

They're manageable, sustainable, and lead to lasting change by building up to significant results.
For example:

- To develop a habit of sleeping better, start by practicing a relaxation technique for 5 minutes each night before bed.
- To form a habit of exercise, try just five minutes of brisk activity each day.

2) Create a "cue" or trigger

- Put a reminder note on your fridge to prompt the habit you're working on.
- Choose a specific time each day to do your walks, such as in the mornings after breakfast.

3) Use a reward to reinforce the habit

- Treat yourself to a healthy snack after your walk, such as a fruit smoothie.
- After a 20-minute workout, engage in a creative activity like painting, writing, or crafting.

4) Be patient, be persistent

- Recognize that the habit will take time to form and stick with it.
- Celebrate the milestones you pass on the way, like when you can do ten minutes of exercise every day instead of five.

Each Lifestyle section in this book includes an 'Action Plan' for you to plan your habits, and log sheets to record your progress.

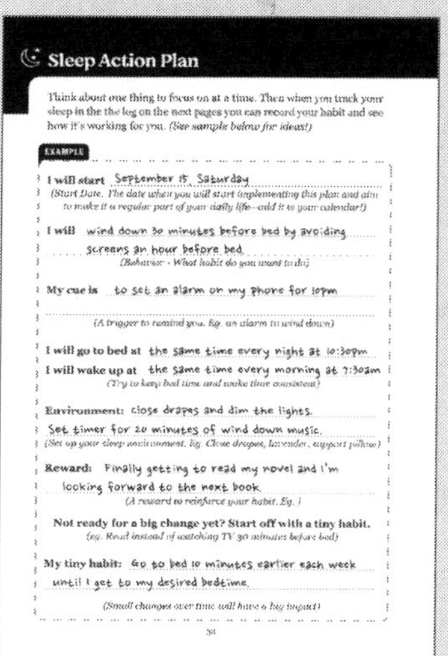

Sleep Action Plan

Think about one thing to focus on at a time. Then when you track your sleep in the the log on the next pages you can record your habit and see how it's working for you. *(See sample below for ideas!)*

EXAMPLE

I will start September 15, Saturday
(Start Date. The date when you will start implementing this plan and aim to make it a regular part of your daily life - add it to your calendar!)

I will wind down 30 minutes before bed by avoiding screens an hour before bed.
(Behavior - What habit do you want to do)

My cue is to set an alarm on my phone for 10pm
(A trigger to remind you. Eg. an alarm to wind down)

I will go to bed at the same time every night at 10:30pm
I will wake up at the same time every morning at 7:30am
(Try to keep bed time and wake time consistent)

Environment: close drapes and dim the lights.
Set timer for 20 minutes of wind down music.
(Set up your sleep environment. Eg. Close drapes, lavender, support pillow)

Reward: Finally getting to read my novel and I'm looking forward to the next book.
(A reward to reinforce your habit. Eg.)

Not ready for a big change yet? Start off with a tiny habit.
(eg. Read instead of watching TV 30 minutes before bed)

My tiny habit: Go to bed 10 minutes earlier each week until I get to my desired bedtime.
(Small changes over time will have a big impact)

31

Part One

Setting the Foundation

You've dedicated countless hours to studying, building your career, and caring for your family. You might even be in charge of your own business, trying to find a balance between work and life that suits you. Your parents are getting older and need increased attention. No matter the path you've taken, life can get hectic and it's easy to lose sight of what truly matters.

Take a moment to reflect. Set aside your never-ending to-do list and reflect on what's really important to you. Dig deep, beyond the superficial. It usually comes down to just a few things.

Maybe it's about spending quality time with your loved ones, having more time and energy for your passions, losing a few pounds, or enjoying better sleep.

Make today all about you and prioritize yourself. As the future remains uncertain, shift your focus from just extending your lifespan to enhancing your health-span. Remember, it's all about you, because being a bit selfish can also be a healthy habit.

A Positive Mindset Matters

Staying positive as you get older is key to a better life. Optimism keeps you healthy and promotes good habits. As you age, a positive attitude helps you make choices that improve your physical health.

Choosing a balanced, nutritious diet is essential for giving your body the nutrients it needs for energy. Exercise can become a fun part of your day rather than a chore. Seeing physical activity as a way to stay active and flexible can improve your health, prevent age-related diseases, and help you take charge of your well-being.

A positive mindset improves how you relate to others. It encourages you to form meaningful relationships and friendships, crucial for emotional health. Strong social ties offer support and enhance your life perspective.

A positive outlook, good nutrition, and regular exercise together create a comprehensive plan for aging well. These practices boost your physical, mental, and emotional health. Keeping a positive attitude is vital for enjoying your later years and leading a full life.

Everything is Connected

Think of your well-being as seven connected pieces: Sleep, Exercise, Nutrition, Alcohol, Physical Health, Mental Well-being, and Friendships. When one is off-balance, it can affect the others. For example, poor sleep can disrupt your mood, while exercise and good nutrition improve it. Too much alcohol or chronic health issues can harm your sleep and mental well-being. Healthy relationships and friendships provide support, but strained ones make everything harder.

So, these factors are like gears in a system. When they work together, you're on the path to a better life. When one gets stuck, it's essential to address it for the whole system to run smoothly.

Is there an area where your life is out of balance?

In the next section, discover more about your overall health and well-being, and identify which areas need your focus.

"THIS SMARTWATCH KNOWS ME TOO WELL -
IT TRACKS MY RUNS, MY SNACKS, AND EVEN SIGHS
DISAPPROVINGLY WHEN I REACH FOR THE REMOTE
INSTEAD OF MY RUNNING SHOES."

Pinpointing Your Health Goals

> *Alone, we can do so little;*
> *together, we can do so much.*
> *—Helen Keller*

You don't have to navigate this path alone, and there's profound strength in that realization. So, consider finding a supportive partner, friend, or family member. Also, cultivate an honest, open relationship with your healthcare professional as you embark on your health journey alongside this workbook.

As a result, by having this support network, you've taken the crucial step—showing up. Now, let's explore your focus for a fulfilling life.

In the following section, you'll assess your current levels of overall well-being across seven key lifestyle areas. This evaluation will help you identify which areas require more of your attention.

Evaluating Your Quality of Life

How do you feel about your current levels of health and happiness?

Write down your replies to the questions below to find out how you're going in each area of your life. At the end of the book, you'll do another assessment to celebrate your progress and identify areas for ongoing improvement. Don't overthink it—just write.

1. SLEEP: Do you sleep well? How are your energy levels during the day?

NO
require meds to "shut off"
thinking - sometimes they dont work
yes - when working energy
is often low

2. EXERCISE: Are you breathless after walking a short distance? Do you feel tired after climbing stairs?

NO
walk 1-2 week
* will go back to OT 1-2 week

3. NUTRITION: Do you eat a balanced and nutritious diet? What would you like to change?

More veggies
good carbs
* vitamins, etc

4. ALCOHOL: Are you drinking more than you should for your health? Do you want to reduce your intake or go alcohol free?

rarely drink

5. PHYSICAL HEALTH: Do you have any chronic conditions, such as: high blood pressure, high cholesterol, arthritis, heart disease, diabetes or other?

NO

6. MENTAL WELL–BEING: Are you practicing self-care and self-compassion? Do you feel a sense of contentment most days?

Not very often

~~w/ friends~~?

7. FRIENDSHIPS: Do you have a supportive network of family and friends? Are you able to connect with others in a meaningful and positive way?

yes, but don't want to reveal tou much or ask to much

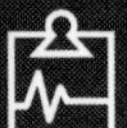

Spinning the Wellness Wheel

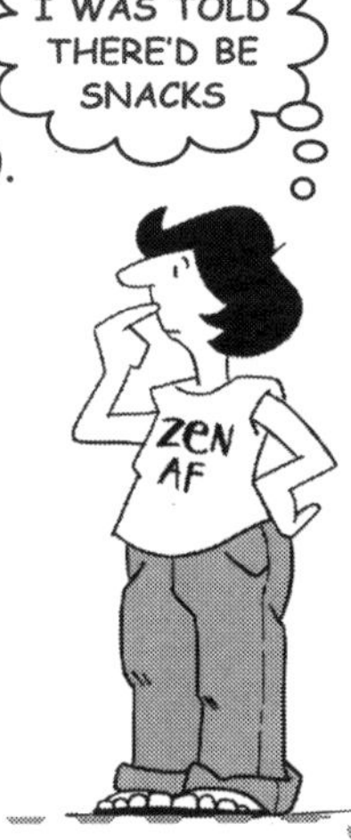

Use this wheel as a tool to visualize your current levels of health and happiness. *Below is an example.*

1) Rate your current level of satisfaction in each lifestyle segment on a scale of 1-10 *(10 being the highest).*

2) Shade in each segment of the wheel according to your satisfaction number.

3) Assess the overall picture, noticing areas where improvement is needed.

4) Implement changes by focusing on the lifestyle sections in this book that you want to improve on.

I WAS TOLD THERE'D BE SNACKS
ZEN AF

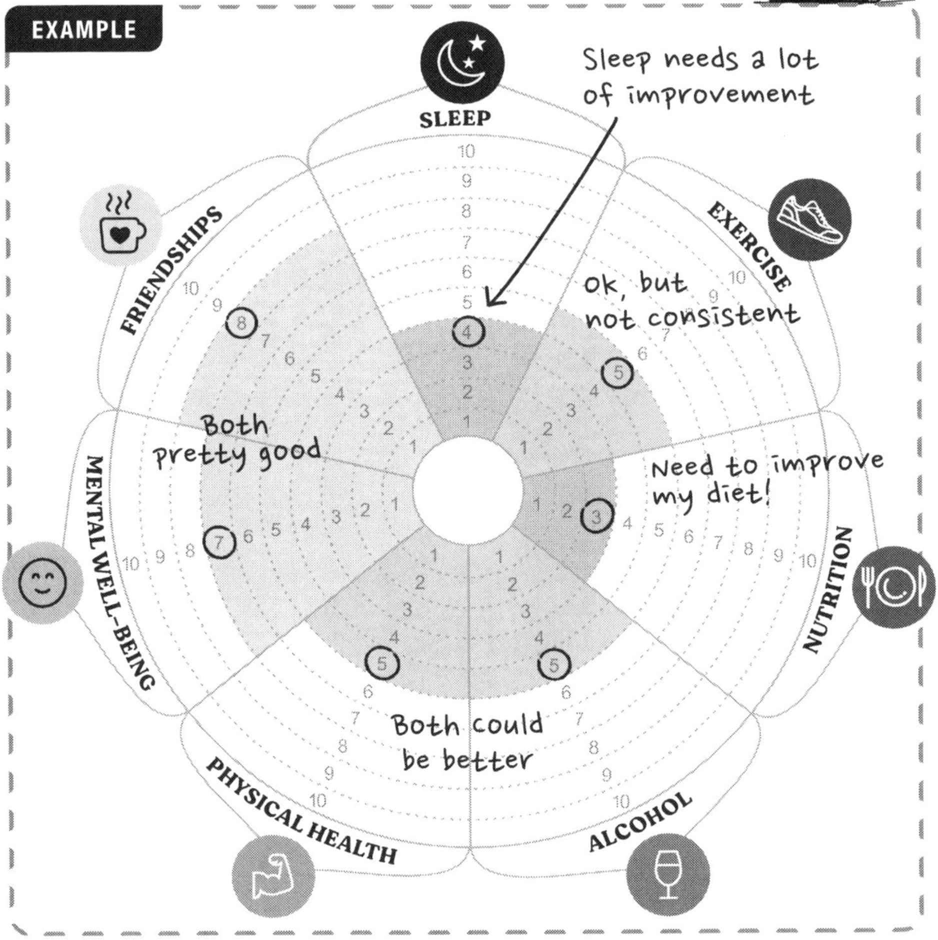

EXAMPLE
SLEEP
EXERCISE
NUTRITION
ALCOHOL
PHYSICAL HEALTH
MENTAL WELL-BEING
FRIENDSHIPS
Sleep needs a lot of improvement
ok, but not consistent
Need to improve my diet!
Both could be better
Both pretty good

Now, over to you...

Add your notes here:

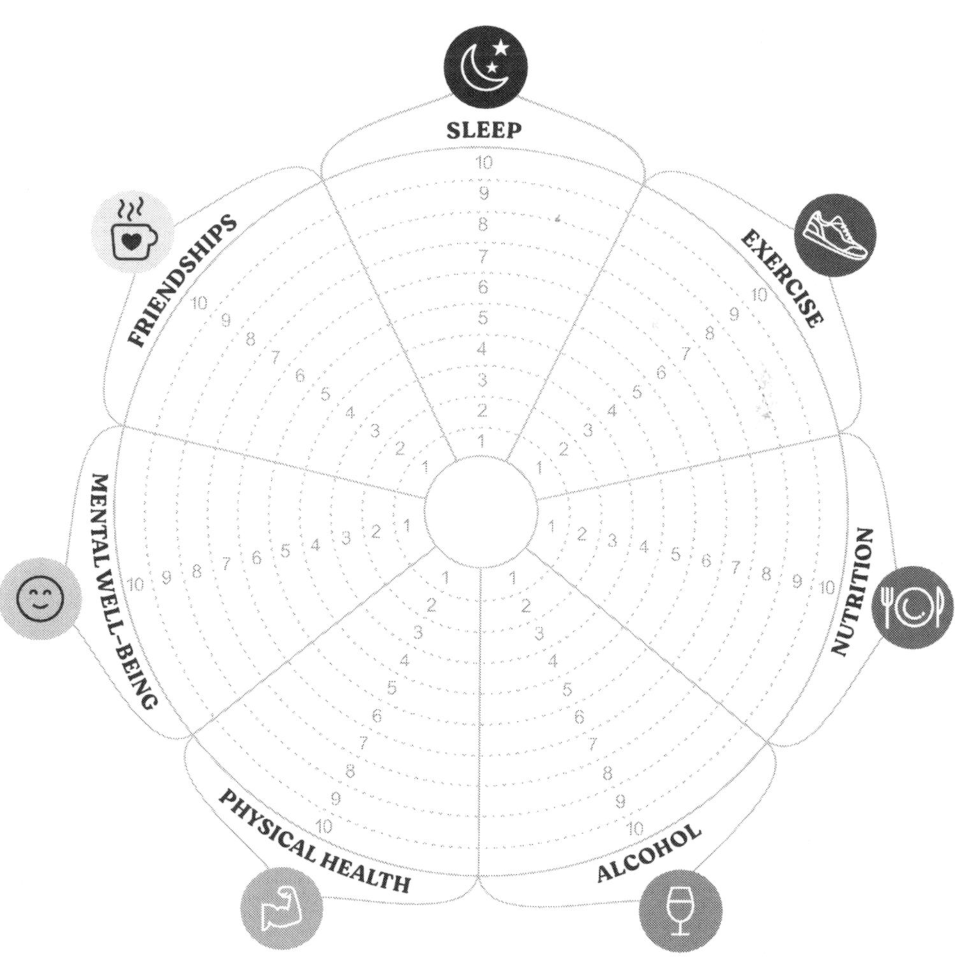

Part Two

The Pillars of Your Health

In Part Two, we explore the seven essential lifestyle habits. Remember, you can always embrace positive change, no matter your current stage in life.

The key is to take small, manageable steps. This workbook provides tools to help you track your growth, reflect on your progress, and celebrate your successes. Let's start this journey together!

"THEY SAY YOU SHOULD FOLLOW YOUR DREAMS. MINE LED ME TO THE FRIDGE FOR A MIDNIGHT SNACK... AGAIN."

HABIT ONE: SLEEP

> *Your bed is a place where you suddenly remember everything you forgot to do.*

You're having trouble getting a good night's sleep. It should be easy, even cats can do it. It may not be every night that you have broken or sleepless nights, but it happens enough to make life unpleasant.

The solution may be simple—or maybe it isn't, but that's why you're here, right?

What may work one night may not work another. The road to sleep is not a straight-line. You are going to have setbacks. The goal is to improve sleep gradually over time. That's where this section can help.

Sleep: *Unlocking the Secrets of Sleep*

Sleep isn't merely a nightly activity; it's a vital part of your life, significantly impacting everything from your body to your brain. During sleep, incredible processes occur within your body, including tissue repair, growth, and mental organization.

Sleep Cycles

Each night, you go through two main types of sleep: NREM and REM. These stages have different jobs that help keep your body and mind healthy. They alternate throughout the night every 90 minutes. Early in the night, NREM sleep is more common, while REM sleep becomes more frequent later. Completing full sleep cycles is crucial for feeling refreshed in the morning.

NREM Sleep (Non-Rapid Eye Movement)

Also called slow-wave sleep, NREM sleep triggers the release of growth hormones. These hormones help muscles absorb the amino acids important for protein synthesis, which supports growth and repair. NREM sleep also aids the immune system in removing damaged cells, crucial for recovering from strain and promoting muscle development.

REM Sleep (Rapid Eye Movement)

During REM sleep, your eyes move rapidly, unlike in NREM sleep where it's deep. REM feels more like being awake. Your brain is highly active, helping with memory, learning, and creativity. It processes emotional memories and new information, often leading to vivid dreams. There's muscle paralysis, a safety measure to prevent physical movement during this stage.

NREM Sleep

(Physical Restoration & Recovery)

It's the time your body heals and grows. Think of it as the body's repair shop, vital for your physical health.

REM Sleep

(Mental Restoration)

It's the period of brain activity. It helps with thinking, learning, and managing emotions.

Understanding the Circadian Rhythm

Your body's internal clock, known as the circadian rhythm, guides when you feel sleepy and when you feel alert. It's a natural system that's been around for a very long time, since before humans even existed.

As life became more complex, so did your internal clock. It not only regulates sleep but also controls when your body releases hormones and when you're most awake. Disruptions to your circadian rhythm can cause sleep problems and affect your health.

Despite your modern lifestyle, your body still follows the basic rules set by your ancestors' circadian rhythms. Paying attention to your internal clock is essential to stay healthy and feel your best.

Working With Your Circadian Rhythm

- **Stick to a Schedule** – Try to go to bed and wake up at the same time every day, even on weekends. Consistency reinforces your body's sleep-wake cycle.

- **Get Morning Sunlight** – Expose yourself to natural sunlight in the morning. Light is the most powerful cue for your circadian rhythm, helping to reset it daily.
- **Limit Evening Light Exposure** – Reduce exposure to bright lights in the evening, especially blue light from screens. Consider using apps that filter blue light or wear glasses that block blue light a few hours before bed.
- **Create a Bedtime Routine** – Develop a relaxing bedtime routine to signal to your body that it's time to wind down. This could include reading, stretching, or meditating.

How Aging Impacts Your Sleep

Your natural sleep cycle can shift dramatically as you age but often fall into two categories, Morning Larks (early risers) and Night Owls.

Young children are often Morning Larks, being awake and active first thing in the morning, and as they age to become teens, they usually shift to becoming Night Owls, favoring later bedtimes and later awakenings.

Once teens grow into adults, their sleep cycles shift again, becoming either category or somewhere in between, often stabilizing for decades until middle age, when sleep cycles steadily shift towards becoming a Morning Lark.

However, genetics can also influence your category. If your family are night owls, you're likely to be one too, even as you age.

So you may have noticed as you age you are growing tired earlier in the day and waking up earlier in the mornings. This is a natural shift, and understanding your current sleep patterns can help to understand when it is the best time for you to sleep and wake as well as know what period of the day you will be most active.

HELPFUL TIP

Siesta Time – Keep It Short & Sweet!

*Taking a power nap can be a good idea if you feel tired during the day or have trouble sleeping at night. Experts say these naps can increase relaxation, reduce fatigue, and improve mood, but keep it short—**about 20 minutes**—before 3 pm, or this can disrupt nighttime sleep.*

Q & A

"How can I improve my ability to fall asleep?"

The key is to unwind and relax about an hour before bedtime. Avoid screens and alcohol; try listening to calming music instead. Stick to a consistent bedtime whenever you can. Your body will gradually adapt to this routine, helping you fall asleep within 20 to 30 minutes. Be patient; it may take several weeks to see improvements.

"How do I get back to sleep after I wake up at 3:00 am"

If you're unable to sleep within 20 minutes, try doing something calming until you feel sleepy. In certain cases, some people find having a relaxing activity or having a small snack before returning to bed helps them get a few more hours of sleep.

I've always had an alcoholic nightcap before bed. Is this a problem?

Alcohol can mess up your sleep routine, especially the crucial REM sleep. While it might seem helpful at first, it can disrupt your rest. It's best to avoid alcohol 2 to 3 hours before bedtime.

"How important is my bedroom temperature?"

You will sleep better if the temperature in your bedroom is cooler, a few degrees lower than during the day. Our bodies naturally cool down at night when we sleep due to our biological patterns shaped by evolution.

"Can using phone and tablet screens impact sleep quality?"

Melatonin, a hormone crucial for regulating our sleep-wake cycle, can be disturbed by the blue light emitted from these screens. Various studies suggest that exposure to such light before bed may interfere with melatonin production, potentially disrupting sleep patterns.

"Is it common to wake up often at night to go pee?"

Frequent nighttime urination is typical, often involving multiple restroom visits. Limiting fluid intake, especially before bedtime, can address this issue. Other causes, including medical conditions (UTIs, diabetes, enlarged prostate), medications, age-related changes, and lifestyle factors, also contribute to this disruption. If you are concerned, seek advice from your doctor.

Simple Tips for a Quality Sleep

If you happen to wake up at 3 am and can't fall back asleep, experts recommend avoiding lying in bed awake for too long. Instead, after about 20 minutes, it's more helpful to get out of bed and do something else until you start feeling drowsy again. Staying in bed awake might make your brain link the bed with sleep troubles.

- **Relaxation Exercises –** To get back in the mood for sleep take slow, deep breaths from your belly. Try a guided meditation or gentle yoga. Another helpful method is progressive muscle relaxation. Start by tensing and then relaxing each body part, starting with your toes and moving up through your body. You can silently say the body part and 'relax' to enhance the effect. *I.e "Toes relax, feet relax..."* and so on.

- **Read or Listen to Music –** Can divert your attention from racing thoughts, promoting relaxation and aiding in falling asleep. Choose gentle, familiar content for reading and soft, slow-tempo music to create a tranquil environment conducive to sleep. Experiment with different genres to find what works best for you.

- **Journaling –** Writing in a journal can reduce nighttime worrying. Just jot down your thoughts about the day and what you need to do tomorrow. Keep a notebook and pen by your bed.

- **Create a Sleep-Friendly Environment –** A dark, quiet and cool bedroom will make it easier to go to bed earlier. Darkness signals to your body that it's time to sleep. Use low-wattage lamps, check for any other sources of light and turn them off.

- **Temperature –** Keep your bedroom around 65°F (about 18°C) at night for the best sleep. A cooler room is thought to mimic the natural drop in body temperature that occurs as part of the body's circadian rhythm when preparing for sleep. This temperature drop helps trigger the release of melatonin, the hormone responsible for promoting sleep.

65°F (18°C)

- **Exercise's Impact on Sleep** – Exercise, when timed right, helps you fall asleep faster, experience deeper and more restful sleep, and have fewer sleep disruptions. Morning or afternoon workouts are especially helpful because they align with the body's natural rhythms and temperature changes. However, engaging in strenuous exercise right before bedtime can make it harder to sleep well. To enjoy the full sleep benefits of exercise, it's important to establish a regular workout routine.

- **Eating Right for a Good Night's Sleep** – The relationship between low and high GI (glycemic index) foods and sleep is tied to their impact on blood sugar levels. Low GI foods, like whole grains and veggies, release energy gradually, promoting stable blood sugar, potentially aiding sleep. High GI foods, such as sugary snacks, lead to rapid blood sugar spikes and crashes, which can disturb sleep by causing wakefulness. Balancing your diet with a mix of low GI foods can support better sleep, but it's also crucial to avoid heavy, large meals near bedtime to enhance sleep quality.

- **Alcohol** – While it may induce drowsiness initially and hasten falling asleep, it later disrupts the sleep cycle. It's generally recommended to avoid consuming alcohol within 3-4 hours of bedtime. This allows your body more time to metabolize and process the alcohol before you go to sleep.

- **Caffeine** – A stimulant found in coffee, tea, energy drinks, protein bars, cocoa, many soft drinks, and some medications. It can interfere with sleep by blocking the action of adenosine, a neurotransmitter that promotes sleepiness. Avoid it at least six hours before bedtime.

- **Nicotine** – It can make it difficult to fall asleep, reduce the overall quality of sleep, lead to more frequent awakenings, and cause withdrawal symptoms during the night. Withdrawal can result in vivid dreams, contributing to sleep disturbances. To improve sleep quality, it's recommend to avoid nicotine, especially close to bedtime, or to consider quitting smoking or reducing nicotine intake.

Evening Routine

A relaxing pre-sleep routine can signal to your body that it's time to wind down. Dim the lights, listen to music, have a hot bath, read or write in a journal. If you struggle to get to sleep, have a longer wind-down time—setting a reminder alarm can be helpful. *See example below.*

EXAMPLE

Time	Activity
9:30pm	Stop watching TV & other electronic devices
10 pm	change into PJ's and brush teeth.
10:30 pm	Dim the lights, put on some relaxing music and
	read my book. unplug from electronic devices
11 pm	close the bedroom drapes.
	5 min. breathing exercise.
	Lights out.

Now, over to you ...

Time	Activity

Morning Routine

Establishing a morning routine promotes a refreshed start to the day. Remember to get some sunlight in the first few hours after waking up as it regulates the body's clock, boosts serotonin, and improves sleep quality. *See example below.*

EXAMPLE

Time	Activity
7 am	Wake up same time each morning.
	Open bedroom drapes, make bed (important!).
7:15 am	Wash face, change into exercise clothes
	5 minutes of light stretching.
8:00 am	Sit out in the garden with a cup of hot water
	with a slice of lemon, mint or ginger
8:30 am	Breakfast
9:30 am	Go for my morning walk

Now, over to you ...

Time	Activity

Sleep Action Plan

Think about one thing to focus on at a time. Then, when you track your sleep in the log on the next pages, you can record your habit and see how it's working for you. *See sample below for ideas!*

EXAMPLE

I will start September 15, Saturday

(Start date: The date when you will start implementing this plan and aim to make it a regular part of your daily life—add it to your calendar!)

I will wind down 30 minutes before bed by avoiding screens an hour before bed.

(Behavior - What habit do you want to do)

My cue is to set an alarm on my phone for 10pm

(A trigger to remind you. Eg. an alarm to wind down)

I will go to bed at the same time every night at 10:30pm

I will wake up at the same time every morning at 7:30am

(Try to keep bed time and wake time consistent)

Environment: close drapes and dim the lights. Set timer for 20 minutes of wind down music.

(Set up your sleep environment. Eg. close drapes, lavender, support pillow)

Reward: Finally getting to read my novel and I'm looking forward to the next book.

(A reward to reinforce your habit. Eg. new pillow)

Not ready for a big change yet? Start off with a tiny habit.

(Eg. read instead of watching TV 30 minutes before bed)

My tiny habit: Go to bed 10 minutes earlier each week until I get to my desired bedtime.

(Small changes over time will have a big impact)

Now, over to you...

Why do you want to improve your sleeping habit?

I will start
(Start date: The date when you will start implementing this plan and aim to make it a regular part of your daily life—add it to your calendar!)

I will

(Behavior - What habit do you want to do)

My cue is

(A trigger to remind you. Eg. an alarm to wind down)

I will go to bed at

I will wake up at
(Try to keep bed time and wake time consistent)

Environment:

(Set up your sleep environment. Eg. close drapes, lavender, support pillow)

Reward:

(A reward to reinforce your habit. Eg. new pillow)

Not ready for a big change yet? Start off with a tiny habit.
(Eg. read instead of watching TV 30 minutes before bed)

My tiny habit:

(Small changes over time will have a big impact)

Sleep Log Improve your sleep quality by keeping a log.

EXAMPLE

Fill out in the morning *(within 3 hours of waking up)*

What time did you turn off the lights to go to sleep last night?
What time did you wake up today?
How many total hours did you sleep *(or try to sleep)* last night?
How many times did you wake up during the night?
Yesterday's factors that might have impacted your sleep quality:
Did you nap yesterday? If yes, what time?
• How long did you nap?
Have caffeine after....3 pm......? *(Write your cut off time. E.g. 3pm)* *[coffee, tea, caffeinated soda, chocolate, energy drinks, certain medications]*
Have alcohol after ......7 pm.......? *(Write your cut off time. E.g. 6pm)*
Have nicotine after ....-.........? *(Write your cut off time. E.g. 6pm)*
Did you exercise?
Eat a heavy meal after ......6 pm..........? *(Write your cut off time. E.g. 6pm)*
Take any sleeping medication? *(Pharmaceutical, Herbal or Botanical)*
• What time and amount of medication?

Date	*Notes*
23rd June	I went to bed later than normal and had a really
	hard time falling asleep. It could have been from
	the alcohol and heavy meal.
25th June	Amazing night sleep! I think the morning walk
	helped and I went to bed on time too.

	Sun	Mon	Tue	Wed	Thu	Fri	Sat
	11:30pm	10:45pm	10:30pm	10:30pm	11pm	11:30pm	10:15pm
	7:30am	8:15am	8 am	8 am	8:30am	8:45am	8 am
	6hrs	7.5 hrs	9 hrs	8 hrs	7 hrs	6.5 hrs	8 hrs
	5	3	1	1	2	4	2
	4pm		4:30pm			1:30pm	
	20min		10min			30min	
	Y/**N**	Y/**N**	Y/**N**	Y/**N**	Y/**N**	**Y**/N	Y/**N**
	Y/N	Y/**N**	Y/**N**	Y/**N**	Y/**N**	Y/**N**	Y/**N**
	~~Y/N~~	~~Y/N~~	~~Y/N~~	~~Y/N~~	~~Y/N~~	~~Y/N~~	~~Y/N~~
	Y/**N**	Y/**N**	**Y**/N	**Y**/N	**Y**/N	Y/**N**	Y/**N**
	Y/N	Y/**N**	Y/**N**	Y/**N**	**Y**/N	**Y**/N	Y/**N**
							Ambien
							11pm.5mg

Rate your sleep quality each night to determine any trends

	Sun	Mon	Tue	Wed	Thu	Fri	Sat
Excellent							
Good			•	•			
Average					•		•
Fair		•					
Poor	•					•	

Sleep Log

Improve your sleep quality by keeping a log.

Fill out in the morning *(within 3 hours of waking up)*
What time did you turn off the lights to go to sleep last night?
What time did you wake up today?
How many total hours did you sleep *(or try to sleep)* last night?
How many times did you wake up during the night?
Yesterday's factors that might have impacted your sleep quality:
Did you nap yesterday? If yes, what time?
• How long did you nap?
Have caffeine after...................? *(Write your cut off time. E.g. 3pm)* *[coffee, tea, caffeinated soda, chocolate, energy drinks, certain medications]*
Have alcohol after ....? *(Write your cut off time. E.g. 6pm)*
Have nicotine after ....? *(Write your cut off time. E.g. 6pm)*
Did you exercise?
Eat a heavy meal after ....? *(Write your cut off time. E.g. 6pm)*
Take any sleeping medication? *(Pharmaceutical, Herbal or Botanical)*
• What time and amount of medication?

Date	*Notes*

	Sun	Mon	Tue	Wed	Thu	Fri	Sat
	Y/N	Y/N	Y/N	Y/N	Y/N	Y/N	Y/N
	Y/N	Y/N	Y/N	Y/N	Y/N	Y/N	Y/N
	Y/N	Y/N	Y/N	Y/N	Y/N	Y/N	Y/N
	Y/N	Y/N	Y/N	Y/N	Y/N	Y/N	Y/N
	Y/N	Y/N	Y/N	Y/N	Y/N	Y/N	Y/N

Rate your sleep quality each night to determine any trends

	Sun	Mon	Tue	Wed	Thu	Fri	Sat
Excellent							
Good							
Average							
Fair							
Poor							

Sleep Log

Improve your sleep quality by keeping a log.

Fill out in the morning *(within 3 hours of waking up)*
What time did you turn off the lights to go to sleep last night?
What time did you wake up today?
How many total hours did you sleep *(or try to sleep)* last night?
How many times did you wake up during the night?
Yesterday's factors that might have impacted your sleep quality:
Did you nap yesterday? If yes, what time?
• How long did you nap?
Have caffeine after...................? *(Write your cut off time. E.g. 3pm)* *[coffee, tea, caffeinated soda, chocolate, energy drinks, certain medications]*
Have alcohol after ....? *(Write your cut off time. E.g. 6pm)*
Have nicotine after ....? *(Write your cut off time. E.g. 6pm)*
Did you exercise?
Eat a heavy meal after ....? *(Write your cut off time. E.g. 6pm)*
Take any sleeping medication? *(Pharmaceutical, Herbal or Botanical)*
• What time and amount of medication?

Date	*Notes*

	Sun	Mon	Tue	Wed	Thu	Fri	Sat
	Y/N	Y/N	Y/N	Y/N	Y/N	Y/N	Y/N
	Y/N	Y/N	Y/N	Y/N	Y/N	Y/N	Y/N
	Y/N	Y/N	Y/N	Y/N	Y/N	Y/N	Y/N
	Y/N	Y/N	Y/N	Y/N	Y/N	Y/N	Y/N
	Y/N	Y/N	Y/N	Y/N	Y/N	Y/N	Y/N

Rate your sleep quality each night to determine any trends

	Sun	Mon	Tue	Wed	Thu	Fri	Sat
Excellent							
Good							
Average							
Fair							
Poor							

What changes could you make to your sleeping place to make it more sleep-friendly?

What are some stressors in your life, and how can you manage or minimize them?

Are there relaxation techniques that resonate with you and that you would like to incorporate?

How would your life be different if you consistently enjoyed a better night's sleep?

Celebrating Successes

What are some positive changes you've noticed in your sleep patterns since starting this journal? How have these changes impacted your daily life?

Lessons from Setbacks

What are some common factors that seem to disrupt your sleep? How can you make adjustments to address these factors and improve your sleep quality?

Notes, reminders & appointments

Date	

Q Questions for your healthcare professional

A Answers from your healthcare professional

“Sweet Dreams, Finally!”

In my younger years, sleep came easily. I'd lay my head on the pillow and drift off without a worry. But hitting my 50s changed everything—falling asleep became a nightly struggle, and staying asleep? Even harder. I felt the effects, from grogginess to irritability, all day long.

A friend suggested that I revamp my nighttime routine, advice that initially seemed daunting but ultimately became my lifeline. The first step was to assess my bedroom environment. I invested in blackout curtains to shield against the bright streetlights. Within a few days, the difference wasn't just physical—it was psychological, signaling to my body that it was time to wind down.

Next, I put a strict rule in place: no electronics in bed. The blue light from my tablet was like a shot of espresso to my brain. Instead, I began a ritual of playing soft, soothing music, which helped mute the day's stresses. Classical pieces, particularly piano, became my lullabies. After a week or so, I noticed I was starting to relax more quickly at bedtime. Creating a consistent bedtime was another game changer. Whether tired or not, 10 pm meant it was time to sleep. This routine helped regulate my body's clock, and over a couple of weeks, my midnight awakenings became less frequent. I also introduced a nightly cup of herbal tea—chamomile or peppermint—and a short meditation or some light reading before bed. These calming activities prepared my mind for rest, easing the transition from the day's activity to night's peace.

Now, my sleep is deeper and more restorative. I wake up more refreshed and ready to tackle the day. These changes, though small individually, cumulatively crafted a nighttime haven that welcomes sleep, rather than mentally wrestling against it.

—Ruth, 65

Bonus Sleep Worksheets

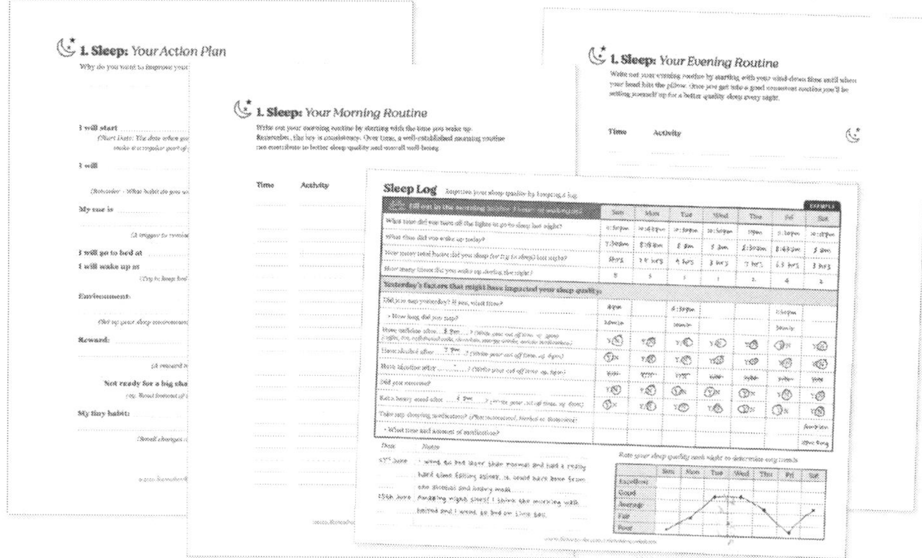

Need more pages to create an action plan or log your habits? Scan the QR code below with your smartphone to get access to free extra content to help you improve your habit.
(See page 2 for how to use QR codes)

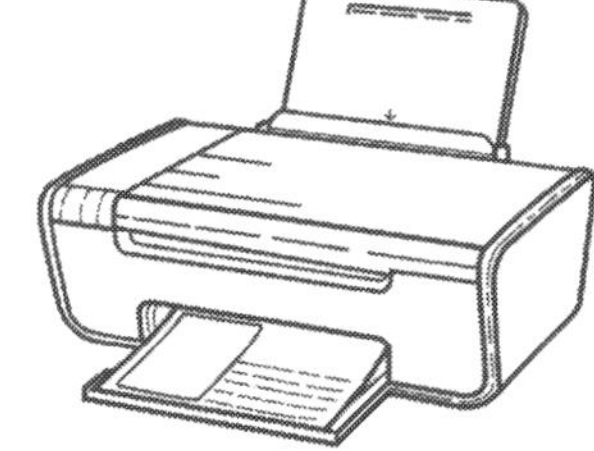

Printables Sheets:

- Evening Routine
- Morning Routine
- Sleep Action Plan
- Sleep Log
- Includes examples

Scan QR code or go to: www.lizalluma.com/after55

Sleep Log Book

Looking for a hassle-free way to track your sleep? The Sleep Log Book is designed to make it easy to uncover patterns and insights about your sleep habits. Whether you're aiming to enhance your rest or simply understand it better, this journal is your go-to tool for better sleep. Scan the QR code or visit **mybook.to/sleep-log-book** to get your copy today!

"IN YOGA, YOU'RE SUPPOSED TO LET GO OF ALL YOUR FEARS. STARTING WITH THE FEAR OF FARTING IN CLASS."

HABIT TWO:
EXERCISE

> *Let exercise be your stress reliever, not food.*

Why do you need to engage in exercise? For many, the thought of exercising while lounging on the couch, thinking, "I will start first thing tomorrow!" remains just an unrealized promise you make day after day.

Unfortunately, there are no natural predators like lions or honey badgers in your daily life to keep you on your toes and healthy. Sure, you may have a significant other to encourage more movement, but wine, doughnuts, or both can easily distract them. Some people are naturals at exercising, but for most, it's a pain. You know it's important, especially as you age, but getting started is a real challenge.

In the following pages, you'll discover why even a modest amount of daily exercise can give you remarkable long-term health benefits.

Exercise and Your Well-Being

When you engage in physical activity, your body releases endorphins, boosting your mood and enhancing mental clarity.

Additionally, your heart benefits too; exercise strengthens it, reduces blood pressure, and improves cholesterol levels, lowering the risk of heart issues. Moreover, regular exercise revs up your metabolism, making weight management easier and fortifying your immune system. At the same time, hormones like insulin and cortisol find balance, contributing to better health, and your bones grow stronger, potentially safeguarding against future problems.

Beyond the physical, exercise acts as a potent stress reliever, enhancing your mental well-being, sleep, and self-esteem. It's a vital weapon in the battle against chronic diseases, promising a longer and healthier life. Furthermore, it can forge valuable social connections.

What Do You Want to Achieve by Exercising?

Your personal reason for exercising will influence the type of exercise you do. Besides making you feel good, below are some common reasons on the importance of physical activity and your health.

Reasons to exercise	
Reduce Stiffness & Increase Mobility	*As we age, if we sit too long, we get stiff and sore. Exercise helps with this.*
Weight Loss	*Carrying extra weight makes everything harder. Walking, sleeping, bending over, climbing stairs & even going to the toilet.*
Organ Health & Chronic Conditions	*Exercise helps with all sorts of conditions, it reduces heart attacks, improves circulation, helps with diabetes, helps combat osteoporosis by improving bone density, and improving mental well-being.*

Q&A

"Can my health conditions stop me from exercising?"
Exercise can often play a crucial role in managing various health conditions, but it's essential to consult your doctor before starting any exercise regimen. They can provide personalized recommendations based on your specific health needs. Don't rule out physical activity completely; it might be adapted to suit your condition and contribute positively to your well-being.

"I feel too tired to exercise!"
It's common to feel fatigued initially, but regular physical activity can paradoxically boost your energy levels over time. Starting might be tough, but it becomes more manageable as your fitness improves.

"I don't feel motivated"
Lack of motivation is a common hurdle, but there are ways to overcome it. Adding a social element to your fitness routine by joining a group or class can make exercising more enjoyable and help you make new friends. Reward yourself for consistently practicing your exercise habits and celebrate your milestones.

"How do I find the time?"
Prioritizing exercise and seamlessly integrating it into your daily routine is key. Try taking a brisk walk during your lunch break, and incorporate micro-exercises like stretching or light weightlifting while waiting for the kettle to boil or your food to cook. Consistency with these small exercises can have a more positive overall impact on your fitness than focusing solely on the duration of a single workout.

"Help! I find modern gym equipment confusing!"
Modern gym equipment can seem intimidating, but most gyms offer guidance on how to use the equipment safely and effectively. Alternatively, you can stick to simpler, classic exercises that require no technology, such as bodyweight exercises or resistance band workouts. The choice is yours; what matters is staying active.

Your only competition is the person you were yesterday.

Exercise Basics

From 5 to 150 Minutes Is Achievable But...

To stay healthy, reaching 150 minutes of exercise per week is essential. Yet, you should not try to hit that target right away, as most people end up giving up. It's better to make small, achievable changes gradually. For instance, start by walking for just 5 minutes every couple of days. This manageable step helps form a long-term habit and gives you an immediate reward, motivating you to continue.

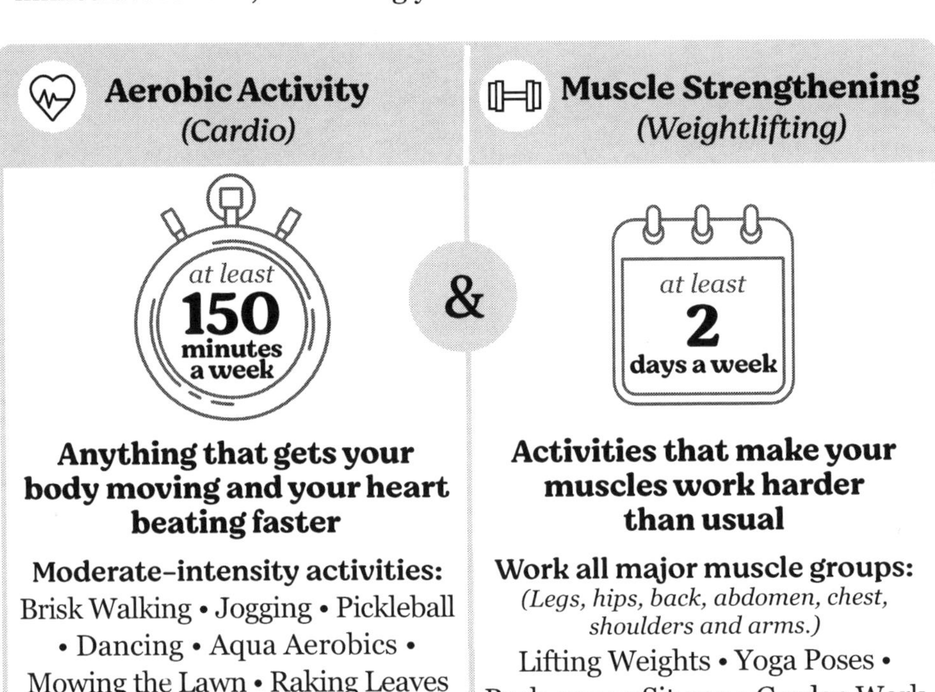

PLUS Balance Training

To help prevent injuries and improve mobility:
Standing on One Foot • Walking Heel-to-toe • Yoga • Walking Backwards • Standing from a Sitting Position

Bone Strengthening

Good bone-strengthening exercises include weight-bearing and resistance exercises: Jogging • Dancing • Power Walking • Carrying groceries • Household chores • Stair Climbing • Tai Chi • Weightlifting • Hiking • Basketball • Fast-paced Aerobics • Squats

Mixing Fun and Fitness

- **Make it a habit** - Think about your typical daily schedule and build in some exercise that's convenient to you. Try not to miss more than two sessions in a row, as it's hard to get back into a routine.

- **Do whatever works for you** - Whether it's a class or a personal trainer, a workout buddy, or your preference for outdoor or home workouts. Choose exercises that are doable, enjoyable and beneficial to your health and you will start to look forward to your activity.

- **Mix it up and learn new exercises** - If you always work out at the gym, see what classes they offer, try a dance class or Tai Chi in the park. Make it fun, make it social!

- **Customize your exercise routine** - Find what suits your own needs, capabilities, and interests. As you age, remember that speed isn't always necessary. You can achieve a great workout by moving slowly but with heightened intensity. For instance, try a leisurely walk up a hill or incorporate light weights into your routine, focusing on perfect form and controlled movements.

- **Choose to walk:** Next time you need to run an errand or catch up with a friend, if the distances are relatively short, opt for walking instead of driving. Take the stairs instead of the elevator.

- **Remember to include balance and flexibility exercises** - You're exercising to extend the quality of your life. Having good balance and flexibility will keep you from breaking your hip by preventing you from falling in the first place.

- **Stretch after your workout** - Your muscles contract during exercise, so it's important to counteract that with stretching afterwards. Incorporating stretching into your fitness routine doesn't need to be time-consuming or complicated. Focus on the major muscle groups you've worked during your exercise session, and hold each stretch for about 15-30 seconds for maximum effectiveness.

Golf: Where even the worst shots are just practice for the next round.

Exercise Action Plan

Define your main exercise goal. What specific outcome do you want to achieve through exercise? Life circumstances and priorities may change, so it's okay to adapt your plan when needed. *Below is an example to give you some inspiration.*

EXAMPLE

I will start Saturday 24th June

(Start date: The date when you will start implementing this plan and aim to make it a regular part of your daily life—add it to your calendar!)

I want to build my strength and flexibility

(Main goal: E.g. improve cardiovascular fitness, build strength, tone muscles increase flexibility and balance)

I will do a weightlifting workout

(Type of exercise or activity that aligns with your main goal: E.g. running, weightlifting, yoga, swimming)

I will do this for 30 **minutes** 2 **days per week**

(Frequency: Decide on the duration of the exercise session. E.g. 30 minutes, 3 days per week.)

I will do this at the local gym

(Location: Identify where you will exercise. Will you exercise at home, a gym, outdoors, or at a specific fitness facility?)

My support buddy is personal trainer at the gym

(Support system: Who could support and motivate you? It could be a workout buddy, a fitness group, or a personal trainer)

Milestone reward: After 4 weeks without missing a session, I'll treat myself to a massage.

(A meaningful reward to reinforce your habit)

Not ready for a big change yet? Start off with a tiny habit.

My tiny habit: I'll take the stairs instead of the lift.

(Small changes over time will have a big impact)

Now, over to you...

Why do you want to exercise more?

EXAMPLE: keep healthy and mobile to stay independent.

I will start ______

(Start date: The date when you will start implementing this plan and aim to make it a regular part of your daily life—add it to your calendar!)

I want to ______

(Main goal: E.g. improve cardiovascular fitness, build strength, tone muscles increase flexibility and balance)

I will ______

(Type of exercise or activity that aligns with your main goal: E.g. running, weightlifting, yoga, swimming)

I will do this for ______ **minutes** ______ **days per week**

(Frequency: Decide on the duration of the exercise session. E.g. 30 minutes, 3 days per week.)

I will do this at ______

(Location: Identify where you will exercise. Will you exercise at home, a gym, outdoors, or at a specific fitness facility?)

My support buddy is ______

(Support system: Who could support and motivate you? It could be a workout buddy, a fitness group, or a personal trainer)

Milestone reward: ______

(A meaningful reward to reinforce your habit)

Not ready for a big change yet? Start off with a tiny habit.

My tiny habit: ______

(Small changes over time will have a big impact)

Exercise Log Track your exercise habit by keeping a log.

EXAMPLE

Activity *Include the type of exercise, location, duration and frequency*	
Description	
walking briskly in the park with Mary 30 minutes, 2 mornings a week	
Duration of activity:	
Aqua aerobics class at the gym 60 minutes, 1 day a week	
Duration of activity:	
Muscle toning at gym with personal trainer, 30min sessions, 2 days a week	
Duration of activity:	
Gardening at home, 60 minutes	
Duration of activity:	
Balance exercises + stretching at home 5 minutes daily after I get up in the morning	
Duration of activity:	

Try to aim for a weekly mix of:
150 minutes of aerobic activity; and
2 days or sessions of muscle-strengthening activity
PLUS Balance training exercises daily

*Plan your week to include physical activity throughout the week. Mark both *columns if activities improve both your heart health and muscle strength.*

	Weekly Schedule *The days of the week (or date) for your activities*							*Cardio activity minutes	*Muscle activity sessions
	Mon	Tue	Wed	Thur	Fri	Sat	Sun	♡	🏋
	8 AM ✓		8 AM ✓					60 min.	
	30 minutes	minutes	30 minutes	minutes	minutes	minutes	minutes		
		5 PM ✓						60 min.	1
	minutes	60 minutes	minutes	minutes	minutes	minutes	minutes		
				7 PM ✓		7 PM			2
	minutes	minutes	minutes	30 minutes	minutes	30 minutes	minutes		
								60 min.	1
	minutes	minutes	minutes	minutes	minutes	minutes	60 minutes		
	✓		✓	✓				–	–
	5 minutes	5 minutes	5 minutes	5 minutes	5 minutes	5 minutes	5 minutes		

Milestone Reward:
What's your reward this period?
a massage after 4 weeks

WEEKLY TOTAL	180 minutes	4 sessions

Exercise Log

Track your exercise habit by keeping a log.

Activity *Include the type of exercise, location, duration and frequency*	
Description	
Duration of activity:	
Duration of activity:	
Duration of activity:	
Duration of activity:	
Duration of activity:	

Try to aim for a weekly mix of:
150 minutes of aerobic activity; and
2 days or sessions of muscle-strengthening activity
PLUS Balance training exercises daily

*Plan your week to include physical activity throughout the week. Mark both *columns if activities improve both your heart health and muscle strength.* 

Weekly Schedule

	The days of the week (or date) for your activities							*Cardio activity minutes*	*Muscle activity sessions*
	minutes	*minutes*	*minutes*	*minutes*	*minutes*	*minutes*	*minutes*		
	minutes	*minutes*	*minutes*	*minutes*	*minutes*	*minutes*	*minutes*		
	minutes	*minutes*	*minutes*	*minutes*	*minutes*	*minutes*	*minutes*		
	minutes	*minutes*	*minutes*	*minutes*	*minutes*	*minutes*	*minutes*		
	minutes	*minutes*	*minutes*	*minutes*	*minutes*	*minutes*	*minutes*		

Milestone Reward:
What's your reward this period?

WEEKLY TOTAL	*minutes*	*sessions*

Exercise Log

Track your exercise habit by keeping a log.

Activity *Include the type of exercise, location, duration and frequency*	
Description	
Duration of activity:	
Duration of activity:	
Duration of activity:	
Duration of activity:	
Duration of activity:	

Try to aim for a weekly mix of:
150 minutes of aerobic activity; and
2 days or sessions of muscle-strengthening activity
PLUS Balance training exercises daily

*Plan your week to include physical activity throughout the week. Mark both *columns if activities improve both your heart health and muscle strength.*

	Weekly Schedule							*Cardio activity minutes*	*Muscle activity sessions*
	The days of the week (or date) for your activities								
	minutes	*minutes*	*minutes*	*minutes*	*minutes*	*minutes*	*minutes*		
	minutes	*minutes*	*minutes*	*minutes*	*minutes*	*minutes*	*minutes*		
	minutes	*minutes*	*minutes*	*minutes*	*minutes*	*minutes*	*minutes*		
	minutes	*minutes*	*minutes*	*minutes*	*minutes*	*minutes*	*minutes*		
	minutes	*minutes*	*minutes*	*minutes*	*minutes*	*minutes*	*minutes*		

Milestone Reward: What's your reward this period?	**WEEKLY TOTAL**	*minutes*	*sessions*

Exercise Journal

What types of physical activity do you enjoy? What are some new activities you'd like try but haven't yet?

How can you gradually add more movement into your daily routine?

Are there any medical conditions that require modifications to your exercise plan?

How do you imagine your life transforming with a commitment to regular exercise?

Celebrating Successes

What physical milestones have you reached since starting this journal? How have these achievements made you feel?

Lessons from Setbacks

What are some common barriers that prevent you from exercising regularly? How can you overcome these barriers and stay on track with your fitness goals?

Notes, reminders & appointments

Date	

Q Questions for your healthcare professional

A Answers from your healthcare professional

Write down your thoughts & feelings about your progress

“Late Start, Lasting Health”

At 56, I knew I was no spring chicken and starting an exercise routine seemed as daunting as climbing Everest. With a family history of heart disease and diabetes staring me down, and my own energy levels in the dumps, it was clear I needed a change. That treadmill gathering dust in the garage wasn't going to cut it anymore. My daughter came to the rescue with a suggestion that sounded manageable: "How about we start with daily walks, Dad?" Simple walks. I figured, why not?

Those first few outings were rough. My body protested every step, and I was winded quicker than I'd like to admit. But I stuck with it, rain or shine, mostly because I didn't want to let my daughter down. Slowly but surely, those grueling walks started to get easier. I began to enjoy the fresh air, the quiet moments away from the TV, and even the occasional chat with neighbors.

As weeks turned into months, I found myself actually looking forward to our walks. I was walking faster, breathing easier, and yes, even jogging a bit. The changes weren't just physical; I felt sharper, more engaged, and genuinely happier.

A year has passed and I'm down 20 pounds. More importantly, I feel stronger and more vital than I have in years. I'm proud to say I haven't just met my initial goals—I've surpassed them. Exercise isn't just a part of my daily routine now; it's a part of who I am.

All it took was a simple, daily walk to start rewriting my story at 56. It goes to show, you're never too old to change your life.

—David, 57

Bonus Exercise Worksheets

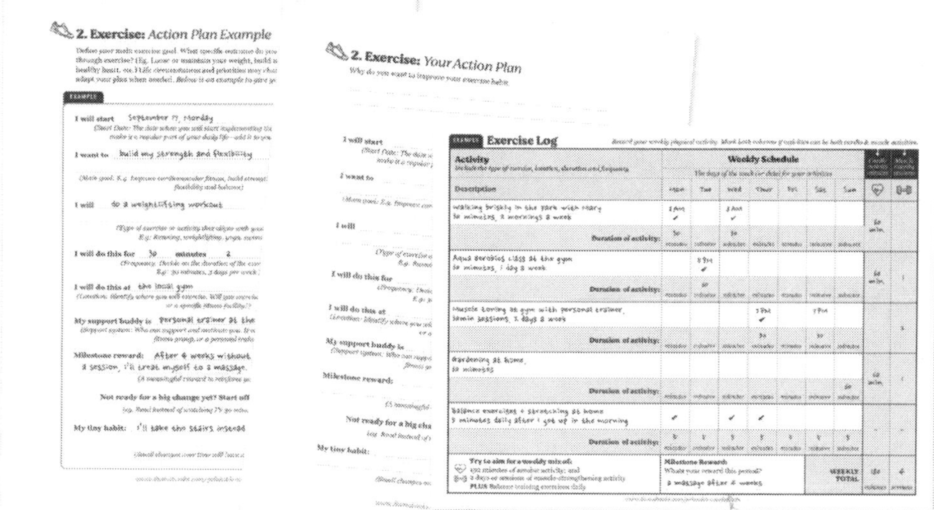

Need more pages to create an action plan or log your habits? Scan the QR code below with your smartphone to get access to free extra content to help you improve your habit.
(See page 2 for how to use QR codes)

Scan me

Printables Sheets:

- Exercise Action Plan
- Exercise Log
- Includes examples

Scan QR code or go to: www.lizalluma.com/after55

Exercise Log Book

Looking for a hassle-free way to track your exercise routine? This log book helps you track your workouts and progress over time, making it easier to stay motivated and reach your fitness goals. Scan the QR code or visit **mybook.to/exercise-log-book** to get your copy today!

Scan me

"YOU KNOW YOU'RE TRULY ADDICTED TO PICKLEBALL WHEN YOU DREAM ABOUT DINKING INSTEAD OF DRINKING."

HABIT THREE: NUTRITION

> *Your body is a high performance engine. Do you want it fueled by kerosene or high octane?*

Some of us have been eating healthily for years, a habit instilled by our parents. However, not everyone has had this advantage. If you're one of those who haven't, now is the time to change your ways, especially if you're over fifty. At this age, a poor diet can significantly impact your health.

Consider these important facts: Heart disease, diabetes, obesity, cancer, osteoporosis, arthritis, and constipation are more common among older adults. This is because as the body ages, it can't repair organs and tissues as effectively. For those over fifty, eating healthily is crucial to manage or even prevent these chronic conditions.

Start with your diet if you're looking to make a significant change in your health. The following pages will guide you on how to carry out these changes.

Nutrition: *Savor Every Bite*

Eating well involves finding a balance in what you eat. It's about giving your body the right nutrients in the right quantities to work its best. It's not about strict rules or depriving yourself, but about making smart choices that keep you healthy in the long run. We've all experienced those 'evil' diet nightmares—fad diets promising the world, only to witness yo-yo weight gain and loss. Improving your diet—both for health and weight loss—comes from small, achievable steps. Say farewell to wasted money on those diet trends and embrace a more sensible approach to eating.

Macronutrients:

Carbohydrates: They provide energy. Choose complex carbs like whole grains and fruits for sustained energy.
Proteins: Essential for building and repairing tissues. Include some dairy, lean meats, fish, nuts, seeds or legumes.
Fats: Important for energy, nutrient absorption, and cell health. Opt for healthy fats like those in avocados, canola oil and olive oil.

Micronutrients:

These are essential vitamins and minerals, like vitamins A, C, D, and calcium, iron, zinc and potassium. They play various roles in keeping your body functioning properly.

Fiber:

Aids digestion, controls weight, and supports heart health and blood sugar. It's found in fruits, vegetables, whole grains, and legumes. Fiber-rich foods keep you fuller for longer.

The Glycemic Index (GI): Rates how quickly different foods raise your blood sugar after you eat them. Picking foods with a lower GI can help manage your energy levels and control your appetite.

High GI foods like sugary cereals and white bread can give you a sudden burst of energy, but can be followed by a crash, leaving you hungry and tired.

Low GI foods like whole grains, fruits and vegetables provide steady energy by slowly raising blood sugar.

Q & A

"What is a healthy diet?"

Common sense advises avoiding fast food and focusing on whole fruits, vegetables, legumes, and grains. Choose foods your great-grandparents would recognize as whole and unprocessed. Reduce your intake of foods and drinks high in added sugars, salt, and saturated fats.

"How can I stick to a healthy diet when I'm so busy?"

Dedicate some time each week to meal planning and preparation. Cook larger batches of healthy meals that you can reheat during busy days. Explore quick and simple recipes that require minimal cooking time.

"How can I prevent overeating?"

Use smaller plates to create the illusion of larger portions visually. Additionally, listen to your body by eating slowly and savoring each bite, allowing time for fullness signals to reduce the likelihood of overeating.

"It's hard to resist cravings for junk food & sweets"

Allow yourself occasional indulgence foods to savor life's pleasures in moderation. Find healthier alternatives to your favorite indulgent foods. For example, opt for dark chocolate instead of milk chocolate.

"I don't always have easy access to healthy food"

Explore local farmers' markets or co-ops for fresh produce and other healthy options. Consider online grocery shopping and delivery services, which may offer a wider variety of foods. Advocate for community programs or initiatives to improve access to healthy foods in your area.

HELPFUL TIP

Healthy Food Subscription Box

Treat yourself to a subscription box that delivers a variety of healthy snacks, ingredients, or meal kits to your doorstep. This can introduce you to new flavors and make healthy eating more exciting and convenient.

What Is a Balanced Diet?

For each meal, eat mostly vegetables, fruit, and whole grains, healthy fats, and healthy proteins. Opt for water instead of sugary beverages.

LOTS OF VEGGIES

- *Dark green, red, orange*
- *Raw/cooked vegetables*
- *Leafy salad greens*

WHOLE GRAINS

- *Whole-wheat bread*
- *Whole-grain pasta*
- *Brown rice, quinoa, oats, rye, barley etc.*
- *Limit white bread & white rice*

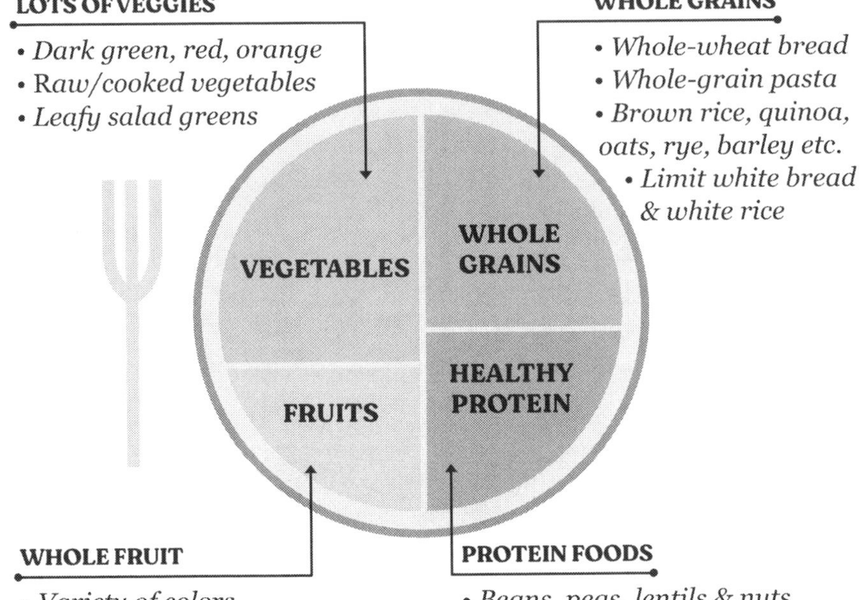

WHOLE FRUIT

- *Variety of colors*
- *Fresh, frozen or dried*

BEVERAGES

- *Water (with lemon slices)*
- *Tea, coffee (limited or no sugar)*
- *Limit juice (1 small glass)*
- *Limit milk/dairy (1-2 servings)*
- *Avoid sugary drinks*

PROTEIN FOODS

- *Beans, peas, lentils & nuts*
- *Fish (salmon & other fatty fish)*
- *Poultry*
- *Limit red meat & cheese*

HEALTHY OILS

- *Olive & canola oil (for cooking & salad)*
- *Limit butter*
- *Avoid trans fat (unhealthy fats found in many processed foods)*

ATTENTION

100% Fruit & Veggie Juices

Try to limit fruit juices, they contain a lot of sugar and not a lot of fiber which is why whole fruits are better for you and just as tasty. One serving of 100% juice can fulfill one of your recommended daily servings of fruits and vegetables, but watch for calories and added sugars or sodium. Choose 100% juice (or 100% juice and water) instead of sweetened juice or juice drinks.

Simple Ideas for Healthy Eating

- **Vary your veggies** - Eat a variety of colorful vegetables—dark green, red and orange. Choose locally grown whenever you can, and eat plenty every day. Add them raw to your salad or cook them in a stew, soup, or a pasta dish.

- **Focus on whole fruits** - Variety is as important as quantity; no single fruit (or vegetable) provides all of the nutrients you need to be healthy. Try whole-grain cereal with your favorite fruit, or add berries to pancakes. *(If you are diabetic take into consideration that different fruits have different levels of sugar.)*

- **Vary your protein routine** - Eating healthy protein sources like beans, nuts, fish, or poultry in place of red meat and processed meat can lower the risk of several diseases and premature death.

- **Make at least half your grains whole grains** - Trade in white rice for whole grains such as barley, bulgur, quinoa, brown rice, and more. Visit your local grocery store's bulk bins to discover new, delicious whole grains that are often simple to prepare.

Hara Hachi Bu (Japanese for 'eating until you're 80% full'): Begin with smaller portions, knowing you can have more if you're still hungry. Using your hand as a guide helps you guess portion sizes without measuring tools. It makes portion control simpler, so you can do it easily at home or when you eat out. Plus, it ensures you have the right mix of protein, carbs, and healthy fats in your meals.

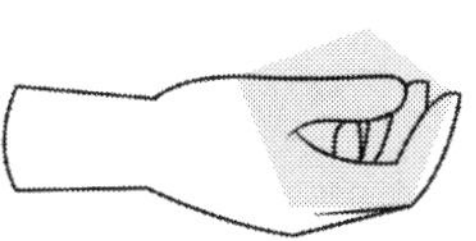

CARBOHYDRATES
A cupped hand

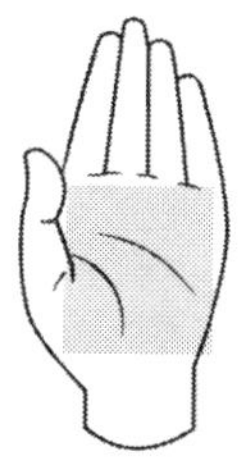

PROTEIN
Palm sized portion

HEALTHY FATS
A thumb's worth

The Body's Need for Hydration

Water makes up about 60% of your body weight. This includes the water within your cells, blood, and between your cells. Staying properly hydrated is crucial for overall health. Water is essential for digestion, circulation, and temperature regulation.

As you age your body's ability to maintain itself slowly breaks down, your vital organs losing efficiency and ability to function properly. The sensation of thirst, kidney function, temperature regulation and many other bodily systems that rely on water are all negatively affected by age, meaning that generally, you need more water than you did when you were younger for your body to continue doing its job, and that you also have a harder time feeling thirsty when you should.

Ideal Water Intake Per Day

The minimum requirement for daily water intake can vary depending on factors such as age, sex, weight, health status, and activity level. However, a general guideline often cited is to aim for at least 8 glasses of water per day, which is roughly 2 liters or half a gallon. This amount may need to be adjusted based on individual needs and circumstances. It's important to listen to your body's signals of thirst and ensure adequate hydration throughout the day. If you have specific health concerns or conditions, it's advisable to consult with a healthcare professional for personalized recommendations.

ATTENTION

Some signs of dehydration

Signs of dehydration can vary in severity, but common symptoms include:

- *Flushed skin*
- *Headache & migraines*
- *Dry lips, mouth & skin*
- *Feeling thirsty & lightheaded*
- *Rapid heartbeat & breathing*
- *Tiredness, dizziness & fainting*
- *Low blood pressure & increased heart rate*
- *Dark yellow urine (should be pale yellow or straw colored)*

Q & A

"I keep forgetting to drink enough water"
Making it a habit to drink a glass of water at specific times, like before meals or when you wake up. Carry a reusable water bottle with you throughout the day. Seeing it can be a great reminder to stay hydrated.

"Is it possible to drink too much water?"
Yes, drinking too much water can cause water intoxication, a condition where excessive water intake leads to an imbalance of sodium in your body. It's rare, but it can result in symptoms like nausea and, in extreme cases, coma or death. Pay attention to your body's signals and drink water when you're thirsty to avoid overconsumption.

"Water is boring!"
Add a squeeze of citrus juice, slices of cucumber, berries or a small dash of 100% fruit juice to your water for a light burst of flavor.

"I crave sweet, bubbly drinks"
Invest in a soda stream and make your own sparkling water. Add a little 100% juice for natural sweetness.

DEBUNKED!

No cheating...

Beer and wine does not count towards daily hydration. Alcohol actually dehydrates the body. (Choose water first but if you want beer or wine, try zero or low alcohol varieties. Alternating water and an alcoholic drink is another option.)

"I can only drink so much water a day"
Add fresh fruits and vegetables that are high in water to your diet such as: cucumbers, oranges, melons, celery, tomatoes, watercress, lettuce and peaches.

"Does coffee or tea count towards hydration?"
Yes, coffee and tea can contribute to your overall daily hydration. While both coffee and tea contain caffeine, which can have a mild diuretic effect (increase urine production), the overall water content in these beverages still outweighs their diuretic effects. Other fluids like milk, juice and soup also count towards your daily fluid intake. It's best to avoid soft drinks and limit drinks with caffeine to three cups per day.

Nutrition Action Plan

Set a specific nutrition goal that you want to achieve. For instance, you might want to eat more fruits and vegetables, cut down on added sugar, drink more water, or include more whole grains in your meals. Your Nutrition Action Plan should match your lifestyle and preferences. *Here's an example to inspire you.*

EXAMPLE

I will start on Monday the 5th of June

(Start date: The date when you will start implementing this plan and aim to make it a regular part of your daily life—add it to your calendar!)

I want to reduce my sugar intake

(Main goal: E.g. vary my proteins, limit sodium intake, increase fiber intake, improve portion control or include more healthy fats.)

I will swap sugary snacks with healthier alternatives, such as fresh fruit, unsweetened yogurt, or nuts.

(Action step: E.g. add a colorful salad or stir-fry into your weekly menu, snack on fresh fruits or raw vegetables instead of processed snacks, read & understand food labels or swap sugary drinks.)

My support buddy is my partner (who does the shopping)

(Support system: It could be a friend, family member, or online community that share similar nutrition goals.)

Milestone Reward: a day at the beach in July

(Reward: E.g. after a month of sticking to my nutrition plan I'll treat myself to a spa day, a new recipe book or cooking class.)

Not ready for a big change yet? Start off with a tiny habit.

(E.g. instead of changing my diet overnight, I'll start with one day per week.)

My tiny habit: have an apple a day instead of fruit juice

(Small changes over time will have a big impact)

Now, over to you...

Why do you want to improve your eating habit?

....

....

....

I will start ....

(Start date: The date when you will start implementing this plan and aim to make it a regular part of your daily life—add it to your calendar!)

I want to ....

(Main goal: E.g. vary my proteins, limit sodium intake, increase fiber intake, improve portion control or include more healthy fats.)

I will ....

....

(Action step: E.g. add a colorful salad or stir-fry into your weekly menu, snack on fresh fruits or raw vegetables instead of processed snacks, read & understand food labels or swap sugary drinks.)

My support buddy is ....

(Support system: It could be a friend, family member, or online community that share similar nutrition goals.)

Milestone Reward: ....

....

(Reward: E.g. after a month of sticking to my nutrition plan I'll treat myself to a spa day, a new recipe book or cooking class.)

Not ready for a big change yet? Start off with a tiny habit.

(E.g. instead of changing my diet overnight, I'll start with one day per week.)

My tiny habit: ....

....

(Small changes over time will have a big impact)

Meal Log

Improve your eating habits by keeping a log.

EXAMPLE

MONDAY	✓ *Tick if this is your indulgence day*
Breakfast	Oatmeal, low-fat milk, berries. Green tea.
Snack	A Peach. Mineral water with lemon.
Lunch	Salmon, broccoli, carrots & brown rice. Water
Snack	3 Digestive biscuits. coffee
Dinner	Green salad, cheese, whole-grain crackers, cold ham. Glass of Low-alcohol wine
Snack	Strawberries & yogurt
TUESDAY	✓ *Tick if this is your indulgence day*
Breakfast	Whole-grain pancakes with fresh fruit & yogurt
Snack	2 digestive biscuits. coffee
Lunch	Tuna salad sandwich with whole-grain bread
Snack	cheese, olives & whole-grain crackers. ½ glass of red wine
Dinner	Quinoa & black bean salad with mixed greens
Snack	Bag of chips, salted nuts & beer
WEDNESDAY	✓ *Tick if this is your indulgence day*
Breakfast	Greek yogurt with granola, fresh fruit salad
Snack	An apple. cup of tea
Lunch	vegetable lasagna, salad & wholegrain bread
Snack	-
Dinner	Baked chicken with sweet potatoes & steamed green beans. Glass of zero-alcohol wine
Snack	2 squares of dark 70% chocolate

✓ Treating yourself to a small to moderate amount of indulgence foods every so often can satisfy cravings and prevent feelings of deprivation.

THURSDAY	*✓ Tick if this is your indulgence day*
Breakfast	Scrambled eggs with whole-grain toast, fresh orange juice
Snack	2 digestive biscuits. coffee
Lunch	Pizza & salad. 1 x beer
Snack	Blueberries & yogurt. Mineral water with lemon
Dinner	Turkey & vegetable stir-fry with brown rice
Snack	–

FRIDAY	*✓ Tick if this is your indulgence day*
Breakfast	Whole grain toast with fig jam, fresh apple juice & coffee
Snack	cherries & mixed nuts/seeds. Herbal tea
Lunch	Beef stew with root vegetables & whole-grain bread. Mineral water with lemon
Snack	Green tea & homemade banana cake
Dinner	Grilled chicken salad. Glass of low-alcohol wine
Snack	–

	SATURDAY *Indulgence day?* ✓	SUNDAY *Indulgence day?*
Breakfast	Whole grain toast, banana, fresh juice	Pancakes, berries
Snack	Yogurt & blueberries	2 oat biscuits. coffee
Lunch	Hamburger, fries & coke	Fish, veggies & wild rice
Snack	cheese & crackers	Homemade carrot cake
Dinner	Baked potato, chili & steamed broccoli	Lentil soup, bread. Red wine
Snack	–	Yogurt

Meal Log

Improve your eating habits by keeping a log.

MONDAY	✓ *Tick if this is your indulgence day*
Breakfast	
Snack	
Lunch	
Snack	
Dinner	
Snack	
TUESDAY	✓ *Tick if this is your indulgence day*
Breakfast	
Snack	
Lunch	
Snack	
Dinner	
Snack	
WEDNESDAY	✓ *Tick if this is your indulgence day*
Breakfast	
Snack	
Lunch	
Snack	
Dinner	
Snack	

✓ Treating yourself to a small to moderate amount of indulgence foods every so often can satisfy cravings and prevent feelings of deprivation.

THURSDAY	*✓ Tick if this is your indulgence day*
Breakfast	
Snack	
Lunch	
Snack	
Dinner	
Snack	

FRIDAY	*✓ Tick if this is your indulgence day*
Breakfast	
Snack	
Lunch	
Snack	
Dinner	
Snack	

SATURDAY *Indulgence day?*	**SUNDAY** *Indulgence day?*
Breakfast	
Snack	
Lunch	
Snack	
Dinner	
Snack	

Meal Log

Improve your eating habits by keeping a log.

MONDAY	✓ *Tick if this is your indulgence day*
Breakfast	
Snack	
Lunch	
Snack	
Dinner	
Snack	

TUESDAY	✓ *Tick if this is your indulgence day*
Breakfast	
Snack	
Lunch	
Snack	
Dinner	
Snack	

WEDNESDAY	✓ *Tick if this is your indulgence day*
Breakfast	
Snack	
Lunch	
Snack	
Dinner	
Snack	

✓ *Treating yourself to a small to moderate amount of indulgence foods every so often can satisfy cravings and prevent feelings of deprivation.*

THURSDAY	✓ *Tick if this is your indulgence day*
Breakfast	
Snack	
Lunch	
Snack	
Dinner	
Snack	

FRIDAY	✓ *Tick if this is your indulgence day*
Breakfast	
Snack	
Lunch	
Snack	
Dinner	
Snack	

SATURDAY *Indulgence day?*	**SUNDAY** *Indulgence day?*
Breakfast	
Snack	
Lunch	
Snack	
Dinner	
Snack	

What are some of your favorite nutritious foods? How do they make you feel?

What are your favorite meals when eating out? How can you make healthier choices when dining out or cooking at home?

Are there any dietary restrictions or considerations based on your health needs?

How would your life transform if you embraced a diet rich in nutritious foods? Describe the positive impact on your daily life and relationships.

Celebrating Successes

What healthier food choices have you made since starting this journal? How have these choices affected your energy levels and overall well-being?

Lessons from Setbacks

What are some common triggers that lead you to make unhealthy food choices? How can you avoid or address these triggers and make better food choices in the future?

Notes, reminders & appointments

Date	

Q Questions for your dietician or nutritionist

A Answers from your dietician or nutritionist

Write down your thoughts & feelings about your progress

“Heartfelt Changes at the Dinner Table”

My husband, Mike, has always been a meat-and-potatoes kind of guy. At 67, his idea of a balanced diet was a steak in each hand. I, on the other hand, have always leaned towards vegetables and grains, especially as we've gotten older and our health needs have become more pressing.

After Mike's last doctor's visit, where his cholesterol levels came back alarmingly high, I knew we needed a change. The doctor had recommended more fish, less red meat, and plenty of fruits and vegetables. Convincing Mike, however, felt like trying to move a mountain.

I started small. For every dinner with steak, I introduced one with salmon. I swapped his beloved white potatoes for sweet potatoes, mixed with a bit of cinnamon to sweeten the deal. Instead of sour cream, we used Greek yogurt; for snacks, I replaced chips with sliced apples or pears.

It wasn't easy. There were complaints, some bargaining, and even a few nights when he'd fetch himself a burger just to make a point. But I kept at it, showing him articles about the benefits of a healthy diet, and sharing testimonials from friends who had revitalized their lives this way. Gradually, he started to see the results. His energy levels improved, he lost a few pounds, and even admitted to liking the salmon. Now, he's not only open to trying new foods but also suggests healthy recipes himself.

Looking back, I see it was all about balance and persistence. Changing a lifetime of eating habits doesn't happen overnight, but with steady effort and a lot of love, even the staunchest meat-and-potatoes man can learn to enjoy a greener plate.

—Linda, 65

Bonus Nutrition Worksheets

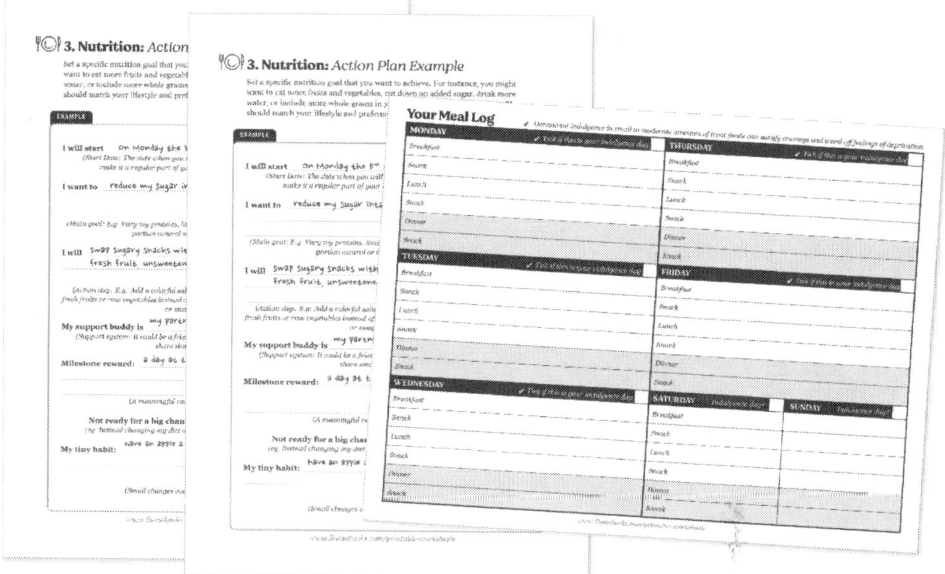

Need more pages to create an action plan or log your habits? Scan the QR code below with your smartphone to get access to free extra content to help you improve your habit.
(See page 2 for how to use QR codes)

Scan me

Printables Sheets:

- Nutrition Action Plan
- Meal Log
- Includes examples

Scan QR code or go to: www.lizalluma.com/after55

Nutrition Log Book

Looking for a hassle-free way to track your daily meals and create balanced eating habits? Whether you're aiming for more energy, weight management, or simply better health, this handy log book helps you stay on track. Scan the QR code or visit **mybook.to/nutrition-log-book** to get your copy today!

Scan me

"WATER TODAY, BECAUSE APPARENTLY, MY LIVER IS NOT AS ENTHUSIASTIC ABOUT WINE WEDNESDAYS AS I AM."

HABIT FOUR:

ALCOHOL

> *Wine is a gift from the gods.*
> *A liquid of beauty and grace.*
> *It can lift your spirits & soothe your soul.*
> *But it can also be your disgrace.*
> *—Unknown*

Alcohol in your youth was lots of good fun with the occasional hangover. It was a social thing, which helped to smooth social occasions and sometimes to reduce stress. At 50+, it's time to discuss excessive drinking.

Common sense tells us that consuming high amounts of alcohol is detrimental to both the mind and body. As you age, your body can become more sensitive to alcohol, increasing the risk of health issues. We are not talking about alcoholism here, which is a whole different concern, but the act of drinking above the recommended daily limit.

"But I love my glass of wine," you say. Read on to find the secret to cutting it down to safe levels.

Understanding Your Limits

Knowing how alcohol impacts your health is vital for making smart choices about how much you drink. When you consume alcohol, it travels through your bloodstream to your brain. This affects the balance of chemicals that control your mood, giving you a temporary sense of calm and relaxation if you drink moderately. But if you drink too much, it can harm your ability to think clearly, remember things, and make good decisions.

Alcohol can impact your health and how long you live. Drinking too much or not following recommended limits can raise the risk of various health problems, like liver disease, heart issues, injuries, and alcohol addiction.

While it may appear to aid in falling asleep quicker, alcohol negatively affects the quality of your sleep. It hinders the production of melatonin and REM sleep, which are essential for falling and staying asleep.

Furthermore, it has the potential to impact your breathing, cause dehydration, raise your heart rate, and decrease heart rate variability, which could lead to daytime fatigue and health issues.

Alcohol Tolerance Declines With Age

Older adults often experience the effects of alcohol more quickly than in their younger years. This change is partly influenced by genetic factors. Additionally, as you age, your body composition changes, with less water and more fat. As a result, alcohol remains in your system longer and has a more pronounced impact.

Alcohol Greatly Affects Mood

While it might make you feel sociable when you're out with friends, excessive consumption can trigger mood swings, depression, and increase susceptibility to mental well-being issues. The way alcohol affects your mood and your thinking is an important factor to think about when you're considering its social benefits.

Q & A

"I just can't seem to reduce my alcohol intake"
The key is taking tiny, minuscule steps. Start by lowering the alcohol percentage in your drinks and sticking with that for weeks or even months. Then gradually make more small reductions, taking it slowly.

"I drink alcohol to reduce stress"
There are other methods to reduce stress. Sports, yoga, very energetic exercise or even learning a totally new skill. Again, reduce your intake slowly when starting new stress reducing methods. Those methods should also be slow.

ATTENTION

Health problems caused by overindulgence

Your brain doesn't stay the same when it comes to alcohol:
Frequent consumption can lead to tolerance, meaning you need more to achieve the same effects. This poses a risk as it may lead you from moderate to heavy drinking without realizing it, potentially resulting in physical and mental addiction.

Chronic diseases: *Diseases such as diabetes, heart disease, liver disease, and osteoporosis can be made worse if combined with too much alcohol. Alcohol can also increase the risk of developing some of these diseases by raising your blood sugar, blood pressure, and cholesterol levels, as well as inflammation in the body.*

Mental well-being: *As we age, excessive drinking can impact memory and mood, raising the risk of accidents and exacerbating conditions like depression and anxiety. Alcohol abuse can initiate a cycle of declining mental health, underscoring the importance of maintaining a healthy relationship with alcohol to safeguard both physical and mental well-being.*

What Is a Standard Drink?

Different types of alcoholic drinks contain varying amounts of alcohol making it tricky to keep track of how much you're actually drinking. Use the servings below as a guide. *(Different countries will vary).*

Examples of how many US standard drinks in each beverage

REGULAR BEER
(can)
5% alcohol
12 fl oz. | 375ml

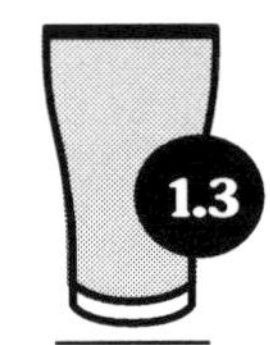

REGULAR BEER
(full pint glass)
5% alcohol
16 fl oz | 473ml

WHITE WINE
(about half a glass)
11.5% alcohol
5 fl oz. | 150ml serving

RED WINE
(about half a glass)
13% alcohol
5 fl oz. | 150ml serving

FORTIFIED WINE
(e.g. sherry, port)
17% alcohol
3.5 oz. | 100ml serving

BRANDY or COGNAC
(single jigger)
40% alcohol
1.5 fl oz. | 44ml

DISTILLED SPIRITS
(e.g. gin, rum, vodka, whiskey)
40% alcohol (80 proof)
1.5 fl oz. | 44ml

As defined by the National Institute on Alcohol Abuse and Alcoholism (NIAAA).

What Is Low-Risk Drinking?

This section is not for people suffering from alcoholism, which is a serious medical condition that needs to be talked about in the proper environment. However, the information here on low-risk drinking can help regular and habitual drinkers reduce the damage to their bodies. It may also assist those considering whether to give up alcohol.

An important factor is drinking water. It helps flush the body of toxins and slows down the process of getting intoxicated. Which brings us to our second tip: The faster you get intoxicated, the more damage you do to your body. Avoid spirits if you can, and if you must drink spirits, use a method of using the same amount of alcohol per drink. It is too easy to make the drink stronger and stronger as you go along. Healthy eating can also lessen the effects of alcohol by restoring essential nutrients. Exercise helps with moods, sleep and stress, and lessens the effects of alcohol abuse.

Low-risk drinking may also take into account the frequency of alcohol consumption. Drinking on most, but not all, days of the week may be considered lower risk compared to daily drinking. Also, everyone's different when it comes to how much alcohol they can handle without risks. What's considered safe for one person might not be the same for someone else.

ATTENTION

The "French Paradox"

Suggests that moderate red wine consumption may be linked to better heart health despite rich diets. But remember, the relationship isn't simple. Enjoying red wine should be weighed against alcohol's risks like addiction and health issues.

Have you tried low-alcohol wines?

Particularly, 8% white wines are quite enjoyable. They give you a little buzz, but drunk in moderation help to reduce your alcohol intake.

Alcohol Action Plan

Set a specific goal that you want to achieve to reduce your alcohol intake. You may want to cut out alcohol completely, switch to low-alcohol drinks or perhaps just work towards reducing your weekly consumption. *Here's an example to inspire you on your path.*

EXAMPLE

I will start today, (September 14)
(Start date: The date when you will start implementing this plan and aim to make it a regular part of your daily life—add it to your calendar!)

I want to drink no more than 2 **drink(s) on any day**

and no more than 10 **drink(s) per week**
(Main goal: Decide how many days a week you want to drink and how many drinks you'll have on those days. It's a good idea to have some days when you don't drink.)

My reason is To have better health as I age
(Motivation: When you cannot avoid a trigger and the urge hits, remind yourself of your reasons for changing your drinking habit.)

I will use this strategy: Start little by little drinking low alcohol drinks over a long period.
(Strategy: Avoid tempting situations by keeping little or no alcohol at home. Choosing low or no-alcohol drinks. Distract yourself with a healthy alternative activity like taking a walk or texting a friend.)

My support buddy is my sister
(Support system: A trusted friend on standby for a phone call, or bring one along for support in situations where you might be tempted to drink.)

Milestone reward: A new book

(Reward: E.g. after 2 weeks of sticking to my plan I'll treat myself to lunch at my favorite restaurant, a new book or exercise gear.)

Not ready for a big change yet? Start off with a tiny habit.

My tiny habit: Non-alcoholic wine at lunch
(Small changes over time will have a big impact.)

Now, over to you...

Why do you want to drink less alcohol?

____

____

____

I will start ______________________________

(Start date: The date when you will start implementing this plan and aim to make it a regular part of your daily life—add it to your calendar!)

I want to drink no more than ________ **drink(s) on any day**

and no more than __________ **drink(s) per week**

(Main goal: Decide how many days a week you want to drink and how many drinks you'll have on those days. It's a good idea to have some days when you don't drink.)

My reason is ______________________________

(Motivation: When you cannot avoid a trigger and the urge hits, remind yourself of your reasons for changing your drinking habit.)

I will use this strategy: ______________________________

____

(Strategy: Avoid tempting situations by keeping little or no alcohol at home. Choosing low or no-alcohol drinks. Distract yourself with a healthy alternative activity like taking a walk or texting a friend.)

My support buddy is ______________________________

(Support system: A trusted friend on standby for a phone call, or bring one along for support in situations where you might be tempted to drink.)

Milestone reward: ______________________________

____

(Reward: E.g. after 2 weeks of sticking to my plan I'll treat myself to lunch at my favorite restaurant, a new book or exercise gear.)

Not ready for a big change yet? Start off with a tiny habit.

My tiny habit: ______________________________

(Small changes over time will have a big impact.)

Alcohol Log Monitor drink count for low-risk drinking.

EXAMPLE

Date *or day of the week*	**Drink Type** *Beer, Wine, Spirit*	**Amount** *Standard drinks*
mon	1 x glass of red wine	1
tues	2 x glass low-alcohol wine	1
wed	½ glass of wine 1 x glass of low-alcohol wine	1
thurs	½ glass of white wine 1 x glass zero-alcohol wine	1/2
fri	1 beer & 2 glasses of wine	3
sat	½ glass of wine 1 x glass of low-alcohol wine	1 & 1/2
sun	ALCOHOL FREE DAY	-
	Total *Number of standard drinks this week*	8

Goal: ***No more than:*** 2 *drinks on any day &* 10 *drinks a week*

External Triggers *People, places, things, times of day, events or special occasions*	**Internal Triggers** *A positive feeling like excitement, a negative one like frustration, or a physical symptom like a headache, tension, or nervousness*
Afternoon, had a long and tiring day	Feeling stressed
Dinner	-
Lunch with friends	-
Dinner	-
Birthday celebration	Excitement, (little guilty)
-	-
-	-

Milestone reward for reaching your goal this week:

A new book

Alcohol Log Monitor drink count for low-risk drinking.

Date *or day of the week*	**Drink Type** *Beer, Wine, Spirit*	**Amount** *Standard drinks*
	Total *Number of standard drinks this week*	

Goal: ***No more than:*** *____drinks on any day & ____drinks a week*

External Triggers *People, places, things, times of day, events or special occasions*	**Internal Triggers** *A positive feeling like excitement, a negative one like frustration, or a physical symptom like a headache, tension, or nervousness*

Milestone reward for reaching your goal this week:

Alcohol Log Monitor drink count for low-risk drinking.

Date *or day of the week*	**Drink Type** *Beer, Wine, Spirit*	**Amount** *Standard drinks*
	Total *Number of standard drinks this week*	

Goal: ***No more than:*** *____drinks on any day & ____drinks a week*

External Triggers *People, places, things, times of day, events or special occasions*	**Internal Triggers** *A positive feeling like excitement, a negative one like frustration, or a physical symptom like a headache, tension, or nervousness*

Milestone reward for reaching your goal this week:

Alcohol Journal

How important is it for you to reduce your alcohol intake? Why?

Have you attempted in the past to stop drinking? If your attempt failed, why do you think this happened?

Do you think you can reduce your level of drinking? Why?

How do you envision your life changing if you were to reduce your alcohol intake?

Celebrating Successes

What strategies have you used to cut back on your alcohol consumption? How have these strategies worked for you?

Lessons from Setbacks

What situations or emotions tend to trigger your urge to drink? How can you cope with these triggers and avoid overindulging in alcohol in the future?

Notes, reminders & appointments

Date	

Q Questions for your healthcare professional

A Answers from your healthcare professional

Write down your thoughts & feelings about your progress

“Family Patterns, Personal Choices”

Growing up, I watched various family members struggle with alcohol. My uncle, my cousin, and most impactful, my father. Their battles cast long shadows over my childhood, and I promised myself I'd tread carefully with alcohol.

At 55, I enjoy wine with dinner and occasional happy hours with friends. Recently, however, I began noticing my casual drinks were becoming more frequent. A glass of wine to unwind after work had subtly shifted to two or three. I saw the signs; I knew them well from my father's decline. One evening, while finishing the third glass, I caught my reflection in the kitchen window — it was a sobering moment. The path I was on was all too familiar. That night, I decided it was time to reassess my relationship with alcohol. I wasn't an alcoholic, but I couldn't ignore my genetic predisposition.

I set new rules for myself: wine only on weekends, and social drinking limited to no more than two occasions per month. I swapped out my weekday wine for sparkling water, finding that the ritual of pouring a drink was half the habit. To stay accountable, I started attending a support group for children of alcoholics. Hearing others' stories helped strengthen my resolve.

It's been six months since I made that change. My sleep has improved, I feel more energetic, and my mind is clearer. I enjoy my weekend wines more, appreciating each sip without the lingering worry of losing control.

Reflecting on this journey, I see it not as restriction, but as empowerment. I am choosing a different path than my father, one mindful sip at a time.

—Laura, 55

Bonus Alcohol Worksheets

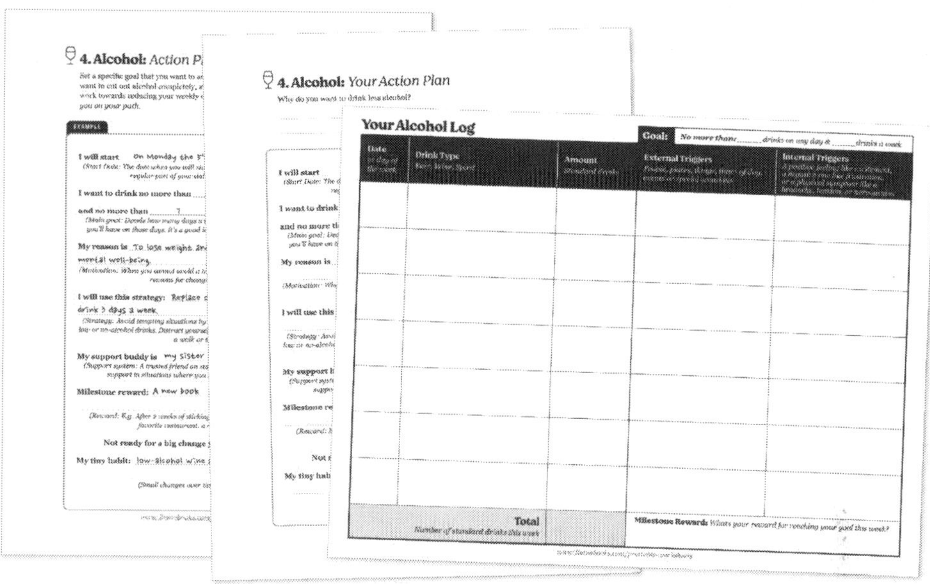

Need more pages to create an action plan or log your habits? Scan the QR code below with your smartphone to get access to free extra content to help you improve your habit.
(See page 2 for how to use QR codes)

Scan me

Printables Sheets:

- Alcohol Action Plan
- Alcohol Log
- Includes examples

Scan QR code or go to: www.lizalluma.com/after55

Alcohol Log Book

Looking for a hassle-free way to cut back on alcohol or simply be more mindful of your drinking habits? The Alcohol Log Book helps you track your intake and see your progress over time. Scan the QR code or visit **mybook.to/alcohol-log-book** to get your copy today!

Scan me

"BOTH DR GOOGLE AND WEB MD SUGGESTED IT MIGHT BE A RARE TROPICAL DISEASE... OR POSSIBLY JUST A COLD. I'M HERE FOR A THIRD OPINION, PREFERABLY ONE LESS...EXOTIC."

HABIT FIVE:
PHYSICAL HEALTH

> *The best gift that you can give your family is a healthy you.*

Even if you're healthy now, it's wise to look after your physical health to avoid future problems. As you age, your body changes and can no longer repair itself as quickly. Engaging in sensible activities now could make for a comfortable retirement.

Consequently, to maintain your health after 50, it's crucial to adopt a lifestyle that includes regular physical activity, a balanced diet, no smoking, moderate alcohol intake, stress management, and sufficient sleep. Sounds challenging, doesn't it? Making minor adjustments gradually is the key.

To help you get started, the following pages will provide a recipe and the ingredients to make it all happen.

Thriving for Longer

As you hit your mid-fifties and beyond, you're probably becoming quite the connoisseur of life's minor aches and pains. It seems like every chat with friends turns into a medical symposium, with each of you sharing your latest health saga. But hey, it's all part of the aging package, right?

Now, you know that with age comes wisdom... and a few extra visits to the doctor's office. It's essential for you to keep an eye out for any signs that your body might be sending you and to have those conversations with your healthcare provider. Think of it as your own personal health summit—a chance to strategize and stay ahead of the game. As you navigate the waters of aging, remember that life isn't just about adding years to your life; it's about adding life to your years.

But fear not! Despite the march of time, you can still be the captain of your own health ship. Maintaining a positive outlook, staying active, and eating well aren't just beneficial for the body; they're good for the soul too. And a little laughter along the way hurt no one—except maybe when you're trying to do those yoga poses!

Boost Your Immune System

The following habits are essential for staying healthy and warding off infections. By incorporating them into your lifestyle, you can strengthen your immune system and improve your overall health.

- *Stay hydrated and get regular exercise to support immune function.*
- *Prioritize getting enough quality sleep and managing stress.*
- *Maintain a healthy gut microbiome by eating a diet rich in fibers, fermented foods, and probiotics to protect against pathogens.*
- *Practice good hygiene, limit alcohol intake, and avoid smoking.*
- *Stay up-to-date with vaccinations and consider immune-boosting supplements under the guidance of a healthcare professional.*

Q&A

"What is a healthy weight?"

Despite efforts by the media to shift your focus from thinness, many people still aim to achieve a low body weight. Yet, using weight as the sole measure of well-being is too simplistic, especially as you age. Moving away from the thinness ideal can be tough, and keeping weight off is even harder. Instead, adopting dietary changes to improve well-being, rather than just losing weight, may be a more sustainable approach. Additionally, for older adults in the obese range, seeking advice from a doctor who specializes in weight management can be very helpful.

"What are the warning signs of potential health issues that I should be aware of?"

Warning signs can vary depending on the specific health issue, but common ones include unexplained weight loss or gain, persistent pain, changes in appetite or sleep patterns, unusual fatigue, and prolonged feelings of sadness or anxiety.

"How do I keep my bones & muscles strong?"

Keep your bones and muscles strong by doing weight-bearing and resistance exercises regularly. Activities like walking, jogging, or dancing are good for keeping bones dense. Exercises such as lifting weights or using resistance bands strengthen muscles. Also, make sure to get enough calcium and vitamin D through your diet or supplements to support bone health.

Additionally, make certain you're getting an adequate amount of protein, which is essential for repairing and building muscles.

"What's the best exercise for a healthy heart?"

Try aerobic activities such as brisk walking, jogging, cycling, swimming, and dancing. Aim for at least 150 minutes of moderate-intensity aerobic exercise weekly, along with activities that strengthen muscles. Always check with a healthcare professional before starting a new exercise routine.

Oops, Not Again! The Leaky Faucet of Life

Older adults often don't drink enough due to decreased thirst sensation with age. Concerns about bladder control or mobility can worsen this. Regular Kegel exercises strengthen urinary muscles, aiding incontinence management when performed consistently.

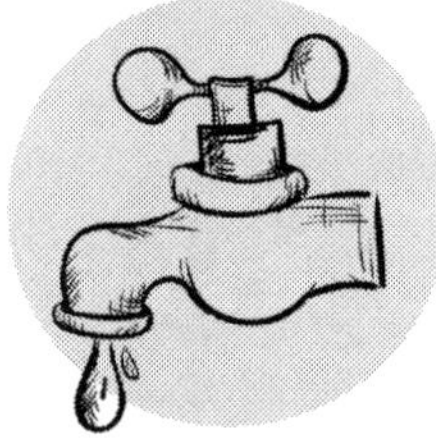

How to perform a Kegel exercise for bladder control:

1) Find the Right Muscles: Identify the muscles you use to stop urination midstream. These are the pelvic floor muscles.

2) Start Position: Sit or lie down comfortably.

3) Contract the Muscles: Squeeze your pelvic floor muscles for about 3 seconds, then relax for 3 seconds.

4) Repeat: Aim for 10-15 repetitions per session.

5) Frequency: Try to do Kegel exercises at least three times a day.

6) Increase Gradually: As your muscles get stronger, gradually increase the duration of each contraction and number of repetitions.

Remember to breathe normally and avoid contracting other muscles, such as those in your abdomen, thighs, or buttocks. If you're unsure whether you're doing Kegels correctly, consult a healthcare professional for guidance.

Night Time Peeing (Nocturia)

As people get older, they tend to wake up more frequently at night to use the bathroom. This condition, known as nocturia, affects about one in three adults over 30 and becomes more common as people age. It happens due to changes in bladder function, hormonal fluctuations, medication use, and the presence of underlying medical conditions. Understanding and managing these factors can improve sleep quality.

Simple Tips for Good Physical Health

- **Trusting your doctor's expertise** is vital when navigating health concerns. While researching health problems online can provide valuable information, it's essential to verify this with your doctor. With years of rigorous medical training and practical experience, your doctor's diagnosis and advice are rooted in global research and scientific methods. Beware of online "experts" peddling exaggerated claims of miraculous cures; if it sounds too good to be true, it likely is.

- **Maintaining open communication** with your healthcare provider is key. Share your health concerns openly, adhere to prescribed medications, and discuss any issues you encounter. If you feel unsatisfied with your current doctor, consider finding one with whom you feel more comfortable and aligned in meeting your healthcare needs.

- **Monitoring your physical health** is crucial. Keep track of any unusual symptoms in the Physical Health Journal provided. This record will be invaluable during your doctor's appointments, enabling you to provide precise details on when and how often symptoms occur.

- **If you have a chronic condition** like diabetes or high blood pressure, effective management is essential. Collaborate closely with your doctor to develop a personalized treatment plan. This may involve medication, lifestyle adjustments, and regular monitoring to keep your condition under control and prevent complications.

HELPFUL TIP

Consider preventive care

These can include things like flu shots and cancer screenings. By doing this, you can help prevent illnesses and catch any potential health problems early. So remember to schedule those appointments with your doctor and communicate openly.

Physical Health Treatment Plan

Fill out and check with your healthcare professional	
Physical Health Medical Condition	
Treatment Period	

GOALS

- ☐ Reduce symptoms related to chronic or medical condition
- ☐ Improve quality of life
- ☐ Increase ability to perform daily activities
- ☐ Other...

LIFESTYLE CHANGES

Dietary Restrictions	
Nutrients high in	

Type of regular physical activity	*Minutes per activity*	*Frequency (per day/week)*

Trigger(s) or environmental factors that may affect the condition

Bring this plan to your healthcare professional for completion together.
Need further personalization? Use the notes section on the next page.

MEDICATIONS			
Medication Name *(Pharmaceutical, Herbal & Botanical)*	Dosage	Frequency	Route of Administration

Healthcare Support Contact Details

Name	
Email	
Phone	
Address	
Name	
Email	
Phone	
Address	
Name	
Email	
Phone	
Address	
Name	
Email	
Phone	
Address	

Physical Health Action Plan

What's one thing you want to improve upon. Perhaps it's managing your diabetes, cholesterol levels, high blood pressure, dental, eye care or menopause symptoms. *Here's an example below.*

EXAMPLE

I will start July 20, Saturday
(Start date: The date when you will start implementing this plan and aim to make it a regular part of your daily life—add it to your calendar!)

I want to improve my blood sugar levels (diabetes)
(Main goal: E.g. improve cardiovascular fitness, build strength, tone muscles increase flexibility and balance)

I will aim to reach a healthy weight with exercise
(Type of exercise or activity that aligns with your Main Goal: E.g. running, weightlifting, yoga, swimming, eating healthier)

I will do this for 30 **minutes** 4 **days per week**
(Frequency: Decide on the duration of the exercise session. E.g. 30 minutes, 3 days per week.)

I will do this at the local gym
(Location: Identify where you will exercise. Will you exercise at home, a gym, outdoors, or a specific fitness facility?)

My support buddy is personal trainer at the gym
(Support system: Who can support and motivate you. It could be a workout buddy, a fitness group, or a personal trainer.)

My Milestone Reward is After three weeks without missing a session I'll treat myself to a massage.
(Reward: E.g. after 2 weeks of sticking to my exercise plan I'll treat myself to a relaxing massage, a new book or exercise gear.)

Not ready for a big change yet? Start off with a tiny habit.

My tiny habit: Spend an hour gardening every week
(Small changes over time will have a big impact.)

Now, over to you...

Why do you want to focus on this part of your physical health?

____

____

____

I will start ______________________________

(Start date: The date when you will start implementing this plan and aim to make it a regular part of your daily life—add it to your calendar!)

I want to ______________________________

(Main goal: E.g. improve cardiovascular fitness, build strength, tone muscles increase flexibility and balance)

I will ______________________________

(Type of exercise or activity that aligns with your Main goal: E.g. running, weightlifting, yoga, swimming, eating healthier)

I will do this for __________ **minutes** __________ **days per week**

(Frequency: Decide on the duration of the exercise session. E.g. 30 minutes, 3 days per week.)

I will do this at ______________________________

(Location: Identify where you will exercise. Will you exercise at home, a gym, outdoors, or a specific fitness facility?)

My support buddy is ______________________________

(Support system: Who can support and motivate you. It could be a workout buddy, a fitness group, or a personal trainer.)

My Milestone Reward is ______________________________

____

(Reward: E.g. after 2 weeks of sticking to my exercise plan I'll treat myself to a relaxing massage, a new book or exercise gear.)

Not ready for a big change yet? Start off with a tiny habit.

My tiny habit: ______________________________

(Small changes over time will have a big impact.)

Physical Health Log

Keep track of your overall health

EXAMPLE

Date *or day of the week*	Sleep *(Hrs)*	Activity *(Type & Duration)*	Fatigue *(1-10)*	Fasting Blood Sugar *(mg/dL)*	Post Meal Blood Sugar *(mg/dL)*
wed	7.5	Jogging 30 min.	3	95/	120
thurs	6	Yoga 1 hr	5	105	140
fri	8	cooling eye mask	2	100	130
sat	7.5	walking 20 min.	4	110	145
sun	7	Gym session 1 hr	2	95	135
mon	6.5	- None today	3	105	130
tues	8	walking with friend. 1 hr	4	98	125

Mood *(1-10)*	**Weight** *(lbs or kg)*	**Blood Pressure** *(Systolic/ Diastolic)*	**Meds Effect**	**Notes & Feelings**
7	150.2	120/80	Nothing noticeable	Feeling energetic
6	149.8	122/78	-	Stressful day (poor diet today)
8	148.5	118/76	Slight headache	Feeling more refreshed after eye mask
5	150	125/82	Upset stomach	Tired in the early evening
9	149.6	118/75	Improved sleep	Excited for the week
7	150.8	122/80	-	Sore muscles
6	149	120/77	Nothing noticeable	Enjoyed nature and our chat

Physical Health Log

Keep track of your overall health

Date *or day of the week*	**Sleep** *(Hrs)*	**Activity** *(Type & Duration)*	**Fatigue** *(1-10)*	**Fasting Blood Sugar** *(mg/dL)*	**Post Meal Blood Sugar** *(mg/dL)*

Discuss the log and any trends with your health care professional.

Mood *(1-10)*	**Weight** *(lbs or kg)*	**Blood Pressure** *(Systolic/ Diastolic)*	**Meds Effect**	**Notes & Feelings**

Physical Health Log

Keep track of your overall health

Date *or day of the week*	**Sleep** *(Hrs)*	**Activity** *(Type & Duration)*	**Fatigue** *(1-10)*	**Fasting Blood Sugar** *(mg/dL)*	**Post Meal Blood Sugar** *(mg/dL)*

Discuss the log and any trends with your health care professional.

Mood *(1-10)*	**Weight** *(lbs or kg)*	**Blood Pressure** *(Systolic/ Diastolic)*	**Meds Effect**	**Notes & Feelings**

Do you have any medical conditions requiring exercise plan adjustments?

When was your last medical check-up, and when is your next one? What steps can you take to ensure you're getting the recommended screenings and vaccinations on time?

Are there any specific health concerns or family history factors that you should discuss with your doctor?

Reflect on how your life would change with improved physical health?

Celebrating Successes

What healthy habits have you developed since starting this journal? How have these habits improved your physical health and well-being?

Lessons from Setbacks

What are some common health challenges you face? How can you work with your healthcare provider to manage these challenges and improve your overall physical health?

Notes, reminders & appointments

Date	

Questions for your healthcare professional

Answers from your healthcare professional

Write down your thoughts & feelings about your progress

"The Lifesaving Lump"

In my early fifties, I prided myself on my health—annual doctor's visits seemed unnecessary. I felt invincible, dismissing minor aches and persistent coughs with over-the-counter remedies. This sense of invulnerability shattered one quiet evening at home when, during a routine self-exam, I felt a small, hard lump in my breast. It seemed insignificant, likely just a cyst, I reassured myself. Concern seemed excessive, so I delayed seeking medical advice.

Weeks passed, but the lump persisted. One night, I mentioned it in passing to my husband. His reaction was sharp and immediate, far from my casual dismissal. His insistence led us to the doctor's office the very next day, where tests confirmed a reality I wasn't prepared to face: breast cancer. The diagnosis was swift, the treatment aggressive. Surgery was scheduled immediately, followed by rounds of chemotherapy that drained my energy but not my spirit. The journey through treatment was fraught with challenges—nausea, fatigue, and moments of deep despair. Yet, with every session, as my body fought, so did my resolve to heal.

Ten years later, I reflect on that time with a profound sense of gratitude. I am healthy, cancer-free, and infinitely wiser. That small lump was not just a call to action; it was a life-saving alarm. This experience taught me the irreplaceable value of listening to my body and the critical importance of early medical intervention. Now, I advocate for regular check-ups—not as mere formalities, but as essential, potentially life-saving measures.

Each year, as I celebrate another year of health, I am reminded of the lesson learned in listening closely and acting swiftly. A simple check-up isn't just routine; it's a key to survival.

—Jane, 63

Bonus Physical Health Worksheets

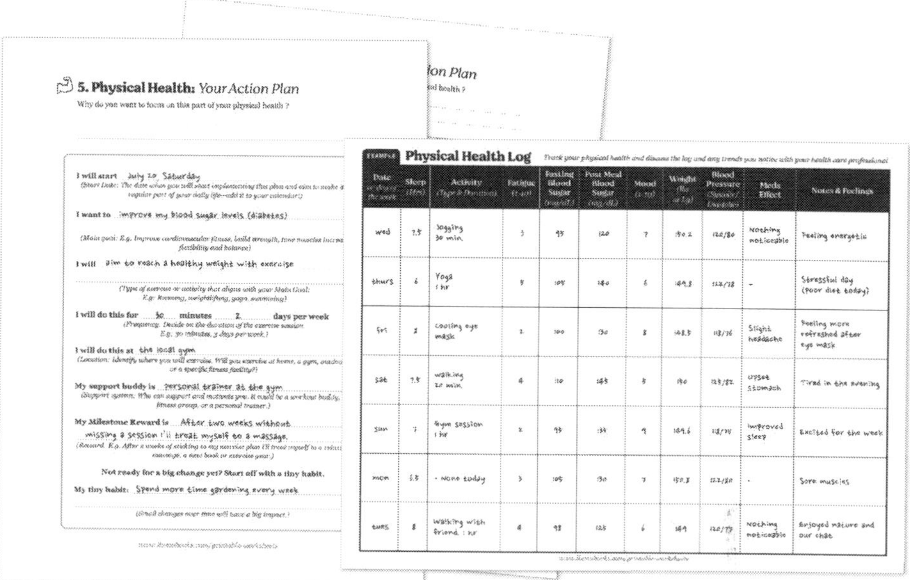

5. **Physical Health:** *Your Action Plan*

Why do you want to focus on this part of your physical health ?

I will start July 20, Saturday

I want to improve my blood sugar levels (diabetes)

I will aim to reach a healthy weight with exercise

I will do this for 30 minutes 2 days per week

I will do this at the local gym

My support buddy is personal trainer at the gym

My Milestone Reward is After two weeks without missing a session I'll treat myself to a massage.

Not ready for a big change yet? Start off with a tiny habit.

My tiny habit: Spend more time gardening every week

(Small changes over time will have a big impact.)

EXAMPLE **Physical Health Log** *Track your physical health and discuss the log and any trends you notice with your health care professional*

Date	Sleep	Activity	Fatigue	Fasting Blood Sugar	Post Meal Blood Sugar	Mood	Weight	Blood Pressure	Meds Effect	Notes & Feelings
wed	7.5	Jogging 30 min	3	95	120	7	150.2	120/80	Nothing noticeable	Feeling energetic
thurs	6	Yoga 1 hr	5	105	140	6	149.8	122/78	-	Stressful day (poor diet today)
fri	8	cooling eye mask	2	100	130	8	148.5	118/76	Slight headache	Feeling more refreshed after eye mask
sat	7.5	walking 20 min	4	110	145	5	150	123/82	upset stomach	Tired in the evening
sun	7	Gym session 1 hr	2	95	135	9	149.6	118/78	improved sleep	Excited for the week
mon	6.5	- None today	3	105	130	7	150.3	122/80	-	Sore muscles
tues	8	Walking with friend 1 hr	4	98	125	6	149	120/77	Nothing noticeable	Enjoyed nature and our chat

Need more pages to create an action plan or log your habits? Scan the QR code below with your smartphone to get access to free extra content to help you improve your habit.
(See page 2 for how to use QR codes)

Scan me

Printables Sheets:

- Physical Health Action Plan
- Physical Health Log
- Includes examples

(Scan QR code or go to: www.lizalluma.com/after55)

Health Log Book

Looking for a hassle-free way to track your vital signs, health metrics, and medical notes in one organized place? This log book helps you manage a condition or simply stay proactive. Scan the QR code or visit **mybook.to/health-log-book** to get your copy today!

Scan me

"JUST CALLED TO ASK IF YOU'VE
SEEN MY PHONE ANYWHERE...
WAIT, NEVER MIND."

Out with the Wrinkles

Press Only Special — $17.49

Start your cruise with freshly pressed clothing — for one low price. Fit up to 10 pieces into the bag provided and leave it for your stateroom attendant. Our clothing professionals will work as quickly as possible to press and return your garments within 48 hours.

Guest Name ______________________ **Stateroom** ____________

Onboard Expense Account ____________________

Item Description	Quantity
Suit	
Dress/Skirt	
Pants/Shorts	
Dress Shirt/T-shirt	
Blouse/Slip	
Jacket/Vest	

Guest Signature ______________________________

Terms: In case of any damage or loss, liability is limited to seven times the price charged for the pressing of said items. Laundry is not responsible for color alteration or faults in the material. Our count must be accepted as correct, unless an itemized list is included. Any claims must be accompanied by itemized list and made within 24 hours of service rendered.

HABIT SIX:

MENTAL WELL-BEING

Health isn't just about what you're eating & doing. It's also about what you're thinking, feeling & saying.

You might find it difficult to discuss mental well-being, especially if you're of a generation where it carried a stigma. However, it's common to have experienced depression, anxiety, or loneliness at some point. It's not a sign of weakness to talk about these issues and seek help. There are many strategies and resources available to help you cope and enhance your mental well-being as you grow older.

In the following pages, you'll start a journey of discovery about the benefits of physical activity, social connection, and mindfulness. It's a journey of hope into your golden years.

 Mental Well-Being: *Daily Harmony*

As you embrace life into and beyond your fifties, it's important to focus on your mental well-being for a fulfilling life. This means managing your emotions, staying strong, keeping your mind sharp, and maintaining social connections.

Take it One Day at a Time

By focusing on the present moment, we free ourselves from the burdens of the past, allowing us to let go and embrace a positive outlook for the future. This approach helps us tackle the stress and anxiety we often encounter in our rapidly changing world.

Furthermore, remember that mental well-being is a personal journey, and what works for one person may not work for another. It's crucial to discover strategies that resonate with you and support your well-being.

Moreover, in times of crisis or significant struggle, don't hesitate to seek help from a mental well-being professional or crisis hotline; support is always available.

REMEMBER

You are not alone

The internet, while sometimes a toxic place, can be a wonderful resource for finding people who share your interests. Online, it doesn't matter what you look like; what matters is what you share and say. Whether your passion lies in photography, collecting bottle caps, muscle cars, or cross-stitching, there's a community for you. These online groups provide a space where you can talk about your hobbies and connect with others who appreciate the same things. This connection can make you feel supported and less isolated, especially if you struggle to find like-minded individuals nearby. Engaging with these communities can enhance your sense of belonging and contribute positively to your mental well-being.

Q&A

"What are the signs of mental well-being issues?"
Symptoms can include changes in mood, thinking, or behavior, such as persistent sadness, excessive worry, feelings of hopelessness, difficulty concentrating, or changes in sleep, appetite, or energy levels.

"How can I manage and reduce my stress levels?"
Practice relaxation techniques like deep breathing, meditation, or yoga. Engage in regular physical activity and ensure you're getting enough quality sleep each night. Maintain a healthy lifestyle by eating a balanced diet, limiting caffeine and alcohol intake, and avoiding tobacco and recreational drugs.

"Is mental illness common?"
Yes, mental illnesses are more common than many people realize. According to the World Health Organization, nearly one in four people worldwide will be affected by a mental or neurological disorder at some point in their lives.

"I don't like my therapist, what should I do?"
Having a good therapist that you can get along with is important. Don't be afraid to shop around if you can, and try out a few different therapists until you find one you are comfortable with.

"Where can I seek help for mental well-being problems?"
While your local GP can be a good starting point, also seek out local government health services. Regardless of the country you're in, most places have national and state-based initiatives that are free for people to access. These services, like our Primary Health Networks or local Health Districts, often commission services or have service lists of providers to which they can direct people. There are also many support groups, hotlines, and online resources available.

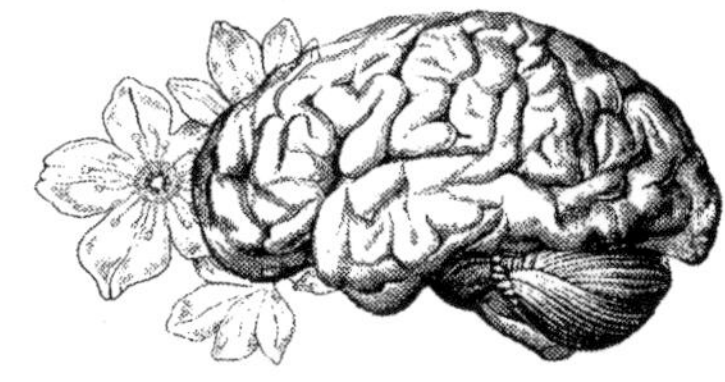

"The greatest weapon against stress is our ability to choose one thought over another." — William James

Tips & Techniques

Cultivate Good Mental Well-Being

- **Support Network** – Staying connected with friends, family, and your community can help you feel supported and reduce feelings of loneliness and isolation.

- **Know Your Local Services** – Maintaining a basic connection and awareness of local support services not only allows you to more readily respond to your own mental well-being needs, but it also provides opportunity for you to support others in their time of need. This reduces your own personal burden while also contributing to the overall well-being of your community.

- **Stress Management** – This is crucial for good mental well-being. Practicing mindfulness, meditation, or deep breathing can help you manage stress and improve your overall well-being.

- **The Power of Gratitude** – Maintaining a gratitude journal can be a unique way to boost mental well-being. Reflect on daily blessings and positive experiences to foster a more positive outlook on life.

- **Art Therapy** – Unleash your creative side to nurture mental well-being. Engaging in art, whether through painting, drawing, or crafting, provides an outlet for self-expression and stress relief.

- **Regular Physical Activity** – Exercise can have a positive impact on your mental well-being and help you maintain good physical health.

- **Humor** – Remember to try to laugh at yourself and find humor in your own mistakes and flaws, while also being kind and compassionate to yourself.

- **Nature Connection** – Spending time in nature has been proven to reduce stress and anxiety. Get your hands dirty in the garden or incorporate eco-therapy by taking regular walks in natural settings.

The 4-7-8 Simple Relaxation Exercise

One popular breathing technique to reduce stress is called the "4-7-8" or "Relaxing Breath" technique.

Here's how it works:

1) Find a quiet and comfortable place to sit or lie down. This could be your favorite spot on the couch, or even your bed.

2) Close your eyes gently and take a deep breath in through your nose, counting silently to four as you inhale. Feel your lungs fill up with air as you breathe in.

3) Hold your breath for a slow count of seven. Allow yourself to fully experience the stillness and peace in this moment.

4) Now, exhale slowly and completely through your mouth for a count of eight. As you exhale, make a gentle whooshing sound, releasing any tension or stress you may be holding onto.

5) That completes one cycle of the 4-7-8 technique. Take a moment to notice how your body feels, perhaps a sense of calm washing over you.

6) Repeat this cycle three more times, for a total of four breath cycles. With each cycle, allow yourself to sink deeper into relaxation.

Practicing the 4-7-8 technique regularly can have profound benefits for your overall well-being. By increasing oxygen levels in your body and calming the nervous system, it helps to reduce stress, anxiety, and tension. Remember, consistency is key, so aim to incorporate this exercise into your daily routine. If you ever feel lightheaded or uncomfortable while practicing, simply return to your normal breathing pattern. Take care of yourself and enjoy the soothing effects of this simple yet powerful relaxation technique.

Mental Well-Being Treatment Plan

Fill out and check with your healthcare professional	
Medical Condition	
Treatment Period	

GOALS

- ☐ Improve mental well-being symptoms
- ☐ Improve quality of life
- ☐ Increase ability to cope with stressors and triggers
- ☐ Other...

LIFESTYLE CHANGES

Dietary Restrictions	
Nutrients high in	

Type of regular physical activity	*Minutes per activity*	*Frequency (per day/week)*

Trigger(s) or environmental factors that may affect the condition

Bring this plan to your healthcare professional for completion together. Need further personalization? Use the notes section on the next page.

MEDICATIONS

Medication Name *(Pharmaceutical, Herbal & Botanical)*	Dosage	Frequency	Route of Administration

Healthcare Support Contact Details

Name	
Email	
Phone	
Address	
Name	
Email	
Phone	
Address	
Name	
Email	
Phone	
Address	
Name	
Email	
Phone	
Address	

Notes about your treatment plan

Mental Well-Being Action Plan

Define your main mental well-being goal. What specific outcome do you want to achieve? Remain flexible to adjusting your plan as needed as circumstances and priorities may change. *See example below.*

EXAMPLE

I will start next Monday, March 20

(Start date: The date when you will start implementing this plan and aim to make it a regular part of your daily life—add it to your calendar!)

I want to practice daily gratitude

(Main goal: Reduce the anxiety I feel and cope with the stress at work.)

If I need a counsellor, it will be: Dr. Amador

(Consult with your regular doctor first to keep him in the loop.)

I will write 3 things I'm grateful for everyday

(Type and location of activity that will help in my main goal: E.g. yoga, meet with supportive friends, go to the gym, journal.)

I will do this for 15 **minutes** 7 **days per week**

(Frequency: Decide on the duration of the activity session. E.g. 30 minutes, 3 days per week.)

My support buddy is veronica

(Support system: Choose a close friend or family member you feel comfortable to share your feelings with.)

My Milestone Reward is a shiatsu massage after 6 weeks of daily journaling

(Reward: E.g. after 2 weeks of sticking to my plan I'll treat myself to a relaxing massage, a new book or exercise gear.)

Not ready for a big change yet? Start off with a tiny habit.

My tiny habit: Being aware of something to be grateful for (no matter how small) - every evening before bed.

(Small changes over time will have a big impact.)

Now, over to you...

What's your main motivation to improve your mental well-being?

____

____

I will start ______________________________

(Start date: The date when you will start implementing this plan and aim to make it a regular part of your daily life—add it to your calendar!)

I want to ______________________________

(Main goal: Reduce the anxiety I feel and cope with the stress at work.)

If I need a counsellor, it will be: ________________

(Consult with your regular doctor first to keep him in the loop.)

I will ______________________________

(Type and location of activity that will help in my main goal: E.g. yoga, meet with supportive friends, go to the gym, journal.)

I will do this for ________ **minutes** ________ **days per week**

(Frequency: Decide on the duration of the activity session. E.g. 30 minutes, 3 days per week.)

My support buddy is ________________________

(Support system: Choose a close friend or family member you feel comfortable to share your feelings with.)

My Milestone Reward is ________________________

____

(Reward: E.g. after 2 weeks of sticking to my plan I'll treat myself to a relaxing massage, a new book or exercise gear.)

Not ready for a big change yet? Start off with a tiny habit.

My tiny habit: ______________________________

____

(Small changes over time will have a big impact.)

Mental Well-Being Log

EXAMPLE

Date or day of the week	Sleep (Hrs)	Activity (Type & Duration)	Mood (1-10)	Meds
10th June	8	Yoga session (60 mins)	6	(Y)/N
11th June	7.5	- None today	4	Y/(N)
12th June	6	Aqua aerobics (45 min)	5	(Y)/N
13th June	8	Gardening	5	(Y)/N
14th June	5	Guided Meditation (30 mins)	7	(Y)/N
15th June	7	- None today	5	(Y)/N
16th June	7	Journaling (10min)	7	(Y)/N

Track your mental well-being. Discuss the log and any trends you notice with your health care professional.

Number of **Positive Interactions**	*Number of* **Negative Interactions**	**Notes & Feelings**
1	0	Woke up feeling a bit low. Work stress contributed. Yoga helped to relax a bit.
0	2	Feeling stressed
3	0	Went to therapy today
0	0	Managed to complete today's tasks.
2	0	Feeling calmer and more focused.
0	2	A bit tired but a good tired - should sleep well.
1	0	It felt good to write down my feelings and what I'm grateful for

Mental Well-Being Log

Date *or day of the week*	Sleep *(Hrs)*	Activity *(Type & Duration)*	Mood *(1-10)*	Meds
				Y/N
				Y/N
				Y/N
				Y/N
				Y/N
				Y/N
				Y/N

Track your mental well-being. Discuss the log and any trends you notice with your health care professional.

Number of **Positive Interactions**	*Number of* **Negative Interactions**	**Notes & Feelings**

Mental Well-Being Log

Date *or day of the week*	Sleep *(Hrs)*	Activity *(Type & Duration)*	Mood *(1-10)*	Meds
				Y/N
				Y/N
				Y/N
				Y/N
				Y/N
				Y/N
				Y/N

Track your mental well-being. Discuss the log and any trends you notice with your health care professional.

Number of **Positive Interactions**	*Number of* **Negative Interactions**	**Notes & Feelings**

Mental Well-Being Journal

What are the main sources of stress in your life right now?

What are some healthy methods you've used in the past to cope with stress?

Who are the people in your life to whom you can turn for support and understanding during stressful times?

Imagine the impact on your life if you prioritized your mental well-being. How might your life improve?

Celebrating Successes

What self-care practices have you incorporated into your routine since starting this journal? How have these practices improved your mental well-being?

Lessons from Setbacks

What are some common stressors in your life? How can you develop healthy coping mechanisms to deal with these stressors and improve your mental resilience?

Notes, reminders & appointments

Date

Q Questions for your healthcare professional

A Answers from your healthcare professional

Write down your thoughts & feelings about your progress

"Quieting the Mind"

For decades, I wore my 'busy badge' with pride. As a project manager in a bustling marketing firm, stress was as natural to me as breathing. I thrived under pressure, or so I thought. But at 57, the relentless pace began to erode my mental peace. Heart palpitations, sleepless nights, and an ever-present sense of dread became my new normal. Anxiety wasn't just knocking at my door; it had moved in.

My breaking point came during a high-stakes meeting when I suddenly couldn't catch my breath. It felt like the room was spinning, and I was the only one losing control. The diagnosis later that week was no surprise: generalized anxiety disorder. My doctor suggested medication, but I yearned for a solution that would help me regain control over my mind, not just mask symptoms.

Reluctantly, I joined a mindfulness meditation class recommended by a friend. The first few sessions were a battle against my own skepticism and the torrent of thoughts about unfinished work. Yet, with each practice, I learned to anchor myself in the present moment, using my breath as a bridge to tranquility.

Encouraged by the subtle improvements in my anxiety levels, I gradually incorporated these mindfulness techniques into daily life. Morning meditations and regular journaling formed my new routine. Gradually, the overwhelming waves of anxiety ebbed. I was not only functioning; I was thriving with a newfound serenity.

Two years later, I not only advocate for mindfulness as a tool for mental wellness but also facilitate sessions to help others in my community find their peace. The journey from chaos to calm has taught me the power of present-moment awareness and the strength of community support.

—Sarah, 59

Bonus Mental Well-Being Worksheets 

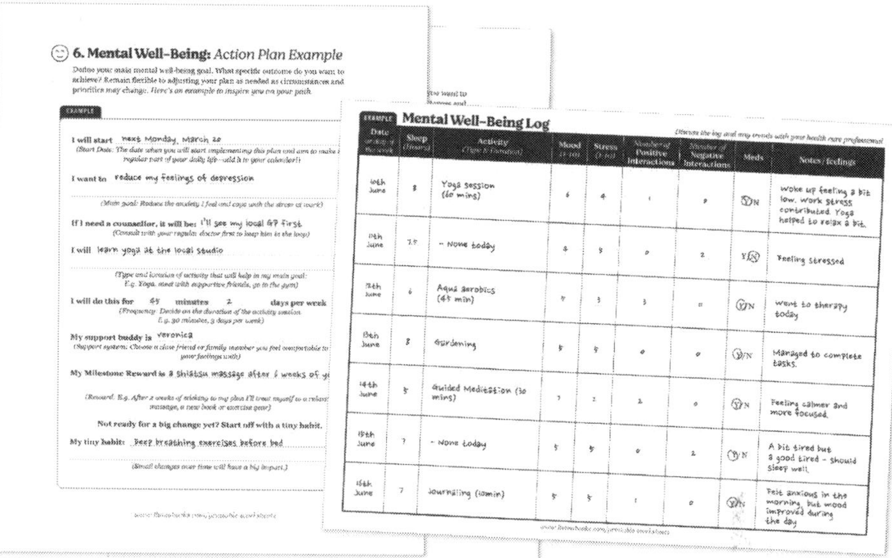

6. Mental Well-Being: *Action Plan Example*

Define your main mental well-being goal. What specific outcome do you want to achieve? Remain flexible to adjusting your plan as needed as circumstances and priorities may change. *Here's an example to inspire you on your path.*

EXAMPLE

I will start next Monday, March 20
(Start Date: The date when you will start implementing this plan and aim to make it regular part of your daily life—add it to your calendar!)

I want to reduce my feelings of depression
(Main goal: Reduce the anxiety I feel and cope with the stress at work)

If I need a counsellor, it will be: I'll see my local GP first.
(Consult with your regular doctor first to keep him in the loop)

I will learn yoga at the local studio
(Type and location of activity that will help in my main goal: E.g. Yoga, meet with supportive friends, go to the gym)

I will do this for 45 minutes 2 days per week
(Frequency: Decide on the duration of the activity session. E.g. 30 minutes, 3 days per week)

My support buddy is Veronica
(Support system: Choose a close friend or family member you feel comfortable to share your feelings with)

My Milestone Reward is a Shiatsu massage after 6 weeks of yoga

(Reward: E.g. After 2 weeks of sticking to my plan I'll treat myself to a relaxing massage, a new book or exercise gear)

Not ready for a big change yet? Start off with a tiny habit.

My tiny habit: Deep breathing exercises before bed
(Small changes over time will have a big impact.)

EXAMPLE **Mental Well-Being Log**

Discuss the log and any trends with your health care professional

Date	Sleep (Hours)	Activity (Type & Duration)	Mood (1-10)	Stress (1-10)	Number of Positive Interactions	Number of Negative Interactions	Meds	Notes / feelings
10th June	8	Yoga session (60 mins)	6	4	1	0	(Y)/N	Woke up feeling a bit low. Work stress contributed. Yoga helped to relax a bit.
11th June	7.5	- None today	4	5	0	2	Y/(N)	Feeling stressed
12th June	6	Aqua aerobics (45 min)	7	3	3	0	(Y)/N	Went to therapy today
13th June	8	Gardening	5	5	0	0	(Y)/N	Managed to complete tasks.
14th June	5	Guided Meditation (30 mins)	7	2	2	0	(Y)/N	Feeling calmer and more focused.
15th June	7	- None today	5	5	0	2	(Y)/N	A bit tired but a good tired - should sleep well.
16th June	7	Journaling (10min)	5	5	1	0	(Y)/N	Felt anxious in the morning, but mood improved during the day

Need more pages to create an action plan or log your habits? Scan the QR code below with your smartphone to get access to free extra content to help you improve your habit.
(See page 2 for how to use QR codes)

Scan me

Printables Sheets:

- Mental Well-Being Action Plan
- Mental Well-Being Log
- Includes examples

Scan QR code or go to: www.lizalluma.com/after55

Mental Wellbeing Log Book

Track your moods and emotional health with ease. Whether you're prioritizing self-care or managing stress, this log book is designed to support your journey toward mental clarity and inner peace. Scan the QR code or visit **mybook.to/wellbeing-log-book** to get your copy today!

Scan me

"YOU KNOW, THE BEST VINTAGE IS AGED FRIENDSHIP
—WITH OR WITHOUT WINE!"

HABIT SEVEN:

FRIENDSHIPS

We'll be friends 'til we're old and senile.
... Then we'll be new friends!

Old age isn't for the faint-hearted (not that you're old), but with laughter and friendship, it can be more enjoyable. Indeed, as you enter your fifties and sixties, you may start to notice issues like high blood pressure, a weakened immune system, and creaking joints. However, research has shown that laughter can have a positive impact on these concerns. Moreover, strong social ties can make you happier and healthier, often leading to a longer life.

In this section, we'll explore how laughter and friendship can enrich your golden years. You'll learn practical ways to laugh more and cultivate deeper friendships. Keep in mind, there's work to be done to make it happen.

Why Adult Friendships Matter

Close friendships and loving partnerships in adulthood offer scientifically-backed benefits. They reduce stress, support emotional well-being, and enhance mental well-being by lowering depression risk and preserving cognitive function. Moreover, these relationships positively impact physical health, extending lifespan, regulating blood pressure, and strengthening the immune system. Spending time with friends or a partner can boost happiness through the release of feel-good neurotransmitters, fostering belonging, and providing resilience in the face of life's challenges.

Q & A

"I've recently gotten divorced or lost my spouse, when is it okay to start dating again?"

After getting divorced or losing a spouse, it's entirely up to you when to start dating again. Ensure you're emotionally ready and not rushing into anything. Seek support from family, friends, or a grief counselor if needed.

"How do I meet potential romantic partners?"

Meeting potential romantic partners can be done through clubs, hobbies, or online dating. Be clear about what you want and prioritize your safety. Use reputable dating websites. It can be useful to ask someone you trust for help if you're new to technology.

HELPFUL TIP

Let's talk about sex!

In discussing sex with your partner, timing and tone are everything. Choose a relaxed and private moment when you're both free from distractions and stress. Approach the conversation with honesty and sensitivity, expressing your feelings without placing blame. It's about sharing what you desire, what you're curious about, and what could enhance intimacy for both of you. Listen to your partner's thoughts and feelings, and remember, this talk is the beginning of an ongoing dialog. Together, you can explore new possibilities and keep the spark alive.

"How can I make new friends at my age? I'm feeling lonely."

Local clubs, meet-up groups, volunteering, or community centers are great places to start.

Deepen Your Existing Friendships

Make time for your friends

Life can get busy, but it's important to make time for your friends. Schedule regular catch-ups, go for morning walks, enjoy a coffee or lunch together, or plan outings and fun activities to share.

Be a good listener

One of the best things you can do to build and maintain a friendship is to be a good listener. Show interest in your friend's life, listen actively, and offer support and encouragement.

Communicate regularly

Stay in touch with your friends by communicating regularly. Text, call, or email them to check in, share news, or just say hello.

Be yourself

Building strong friendships relies on authenticity. Be genuine, openly share your thoughts and feelings, and give your friend the chance to really know who you are.

Show appreciation

Let your friends know how much you value their friendship. Express gratitude, say thank you, and be generous with your compliments.

Be there through thick and thin

A true friend is someone who is there for you through the good times and the bad. Be there to celebrate your friend's successes, and offer support and comfort during difficult times.

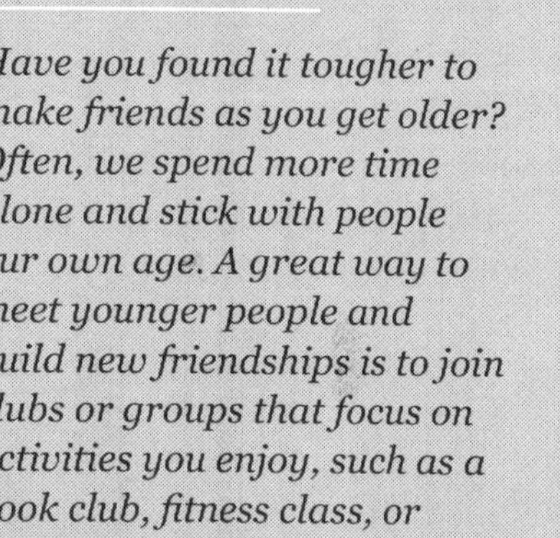

HELPFUL TIP

Loneliness is not much fun

Have you found it tougher to make friends as you get older? Often, we spend more time alone and stick with people our own age. A great way to meet younger people and build new friendships is to join clubs or groups that focus on activities you enjoy, such as a book club, fitness class, or volunteer organization. These shared interests not only provide natural settings for meeting new people but also help spark conversations and connections. Making friends with younger individuals can introduce you to fresh ideas, keep you curious and open, and allow you to share your wisdom and skills. Remember, building trust takes time on both sides.

Animal Companions

How Pets Elevate Your Adult Life

Pets improve your life by lowering stress, encouraging you to be active, and providing emotional support. So, this makes you happier and less lonely. They also give you a sense of responsibility and purpose, which boosts your self-esteem and heart health.

Golden Retrievers and Labradors are known for their friendly and sociable nature, making them excellent companions. Additionally, Beagles and Boxers are reputed for being approachable and having a family-orientated nature. Cats like Ragdolls and Siamese are fond of human interaction, which makes them wonderful furry friends.

Having a pet, especially one from a friendly breed, encourages you to exercise more because you'll need to walk them daily. Pets also help you meet people and reduce loneliness. For instance, if you go to the dog park regularly, you're likely to make friends.

Finally, caring for a pet gives you a sense of purpose and can lift your self-esteem and heart health. The support animals give is invaluable, and a four-legged friend enhances overall well-being and life quality. Just to be clear, love your pets, don't LOVE your pets.

"IF YOU CAN'T SLEEP TRY LICKING YOUR TAIL.
IT WORKS FOR ME."

Celebrating Bonds: Special Events List

Remember your friends' and family's special occasions.

Date	Name	Occassion

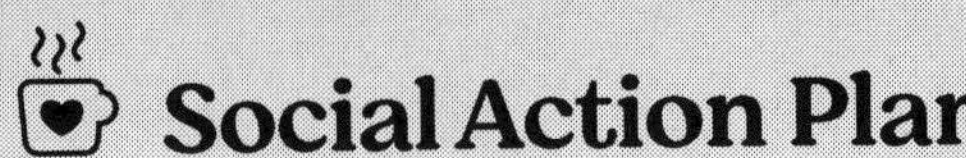

Social Action Plan

A social action plan to become more social and make new friends involves setting specific goals and taking deliberate steps to expand your social circle. *Below is an example for inspiration.*

EXAMPLE

I will start January 10

(Start date: The date when you will start implementing this plan and aim to make it a regular part of your daily life—add it to your calendar!)

I want to find a fitness buddy that likes social walking

(Main goal: E.g. increase my circle of friends to include younger ones with more diverse backgrounds, causal friends, activity partners.)

I will contact my local community center for information of clubs I could join.

(Type of activity that aligns with your main goal: E.g. book clubs, sporting groups.)

My support buddy is Mary

(Support system: Who can support and motivate you. E.g. it could be a counselor, close friend or family member.)

My Milestone Reward is A pair of new walking shoes

(Reward: E.g. after 2 weeks of sticking to my social action I'll treat myself to a relaxing massage, a new book or exercise gear.)

Not ready for a big change yet? Start off with a tiny habit.

My tiny habit: Smile at people more and start up a conversation by complimenting them

(Small changes over time will have a big impact.)

Now, over to you...

Why do you want to improve your social life?

____

____

____

I will start ______________________________

(Start date: The date when you will start implementing this plan and aim to make it a regular part of your daily life—add it to your calendar!)

I want to ______________________________

____

(Main goal: E.g. increase my circle of friends to include younger ones with more diverse backgrounds, causal friends, activity partners.)

I will ______________________________

____

____

(Type of activity that aligns with your main goal: E.g. book clubs, sporting groups.)

My support buddy is ______________________________

(Support system: Who can support and motivate you. E.g. It could be a counselor, close friend or family member.)

My Milestone Reward is ______________________________

____

(Reward: E.g. after 2 weeks of sticking to my social action I'll treat myself to a relaxing massage, a new book or exercise gear.)

Not ready for a big change yet? Start off with a tiny habit.

My tiny habit: ______________________________

____

(Small changes over time will have a big impact.)

Social Calendar

EXAMPLE **Date** *or day of the week*	**Activity**	**Location**
10th June	Movie night	Mark's House
12th June	Book club	Local Library
13th June	Hiking Trip	Maple Pass Mountain Trail
15th June	Lunch	Emilio's Italian Restaurant
18th June	Yoga	Brunswick community centre
20th July	Game Night	Vivian's house
22nd Aug	Rummikub afternoon	Park Slope cafe

Participants	Duration	Notes
Mark, Montse Lisa, Ruth	3 hours	Great fun! watched "The commitments"
Grace, Pat, Lula, Amelie, Mary	2 hours	Discussed "How to survive the good-life" by Mimmo Linguine
Roma, Alba, Joan, Lisa	6 hours	Amazing views! (buy Shona a b'day gift)
Shona, Jeff, Pam, Brian, Russ, clorina	2 hours	celebrated Shona's birthday
Ruth, Jackie	1 hour	New instructor this week.
Lisa, viv, val, Dionne, RJ	4 hours	Played Trivial Pursuit. viv won again! (I think she cheats. Lol)
Michael, Brian, Liza, Sam, Pam	2 hours	Introduced Samuel to the game

Social Calendar

Date *or day of the week*	**Activity**	**Location**

Participants	Duration	Notes

Social Calendar

Date *or day of the week*	**Activity**	**Location**

Participants	Duration	Notes

Friendship Journal

What makes your closest friendship special to you?

Reflect on a recent relationship challenge and what you learned from it.

How do you express love and appreciation in your relationships?

Reflect on the importance of nurturing your friendships. How would you feel if you were supported, understood, and fulfilled socially?

Celebrating Successes

What new social connections have you made since starting this journal? How have these connections enriched your life?

Lessons from Setbacks

What are some common obstacles that prevent you from socializing? How can you build stronger social connections in the future?

Notes, reminders & appointments

Date

Q Questions for your healthcare professional

A Answers from your healthcare professional

Write down your thoughts & feelings about your progress

"Gardening Through Grief"

When Tom, my best friend, passed away last winter, the void he left was palpable. We had spent countless mornings solving the world's problems over coffee, and suddenly, I was alone, the other half of our duo gone. At 68, the silence of my home felt overwhelming.

In the midst of my grief, I stumbled upon a flyer for a local community gardening club. On a whim, I decided to attend a meeting. There, amidst the fragrant rows of flowers and vegetables, I found an unexpected source of solace and companionship.

Sue, who was 72 and had hands stained with soil from years of tending her garden, welcomed me with open arms and a ready smile. She introduced me to John, a compost aficionado, who quickly took me under his wing. The community garden became a place of healing. As my hands worked the earth, my heart began to mend from the loss of Tom. We often lingered after our gardening sessions, sharing coffee and stories at a nearby cafe. This new routine didn't erase the pain of Tom's absence, but it introduced me to different perspectives and new friends navigating their own journeys of loss and recovery.

Each visit to the garden strengthened my connections with my new friends and with life itself. I found joy in the blooms of the flowers and in the laughter of good company. Tom would have loved this place, I thought one day as a butterfly landed softly on my sleeve, a gentle reminder of friendship's enduring presence.

Joining the gardening club gave me a second family and taught me an invaluable lesson: even in loss, there is potential for new growth and new beginnings. The empty chair at our table still reminds me of Tom, but now it also symbolizes hope—for memories cherished and new friendships yet to bloom.

—Michael, 68

Bonus Friendship Worksheets

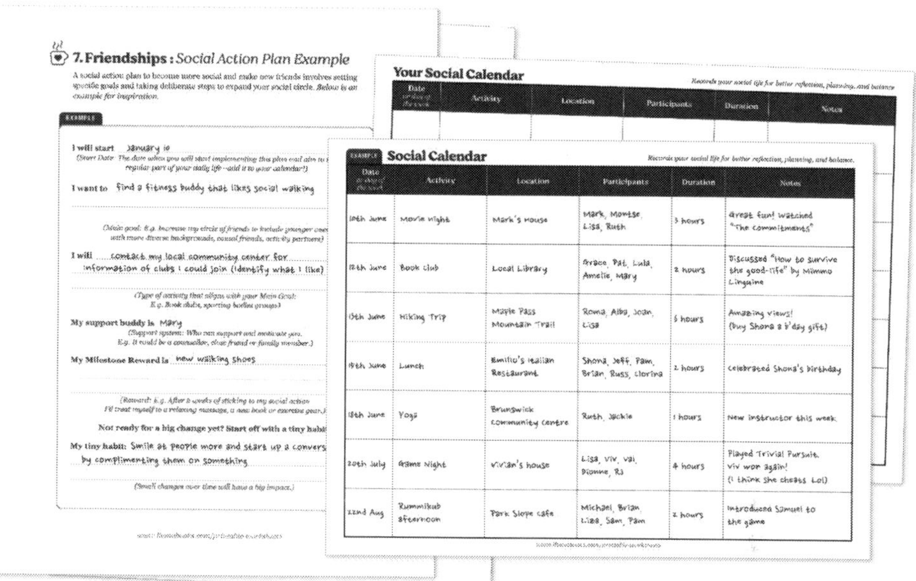

7. Friendships : *Social Action Plan Example*

A social action plan to become more social and make new friends involves setting specific goals and taking deliberate steps to expand your social circle. *Below is an example for inspiration.*

EXAMPLE

I will start January 10

(Start Date: The date when you will start implementing this plan and aim to [...] regular part of your daily life—add it to your calendar!)

I want to find a fitness buddy that likes social walking

(Main goal: E.g. Increase my circle of friends to include younger ones with more diverse backgrounds, casual friends, activity partners)

I will contact my local community center for information of clubs I could join (identify what I like)

(Type of activity that aligns with your Main Goal: E.g. Book clubs, sporting bodies groups)

My support buddy is Mary

(Support system: Who can support and motivate you. E.g. It could be a counsellor, close friend or family member.)

My Milestone Reward is new walking shoes

(Reward: E.g. After 8 weeks of sticking to my social action I'll treat myself to a relaxing massage, a new book or exercise gear.)

Not ready for a big change yet? Start off with a tiny habi[t]

My tiny habit: Smile at people more and start up a convers[ation] by complimenting them on something

(Small changes over time will have a big impact.)

Your Social Calendar

Records your social life for better reflection, planning, and balance

Date	Activity	Location	Participants	Duration	Notes

EXAMPLE **Social Calendar**

Records your social life for better reflection, planning, and balance.

Date	Activity	Location	Participants	Duration	Notes
10th June	Movie night	Mark's House	Mark, Montse, Lisa, Ruth	3 hours	Great fun! Watched "The Commitments"
12th June	Book club	Local Library	Grace, Pat, Lula, Amelie, Mary	2 hours	Discussed "How to survive the good-life" by Mimmo Linguine
15th June	Hiking Trip	Maple Pass Mountain Trail	Roma, Alba, Joan, Lisa	5 hours	Amazing views! (buy Shona a b'day gift)
19th June	Lunch	Emilio's Italian Restaurant	Shona, Jeff, Pam, Brian, Russ, Llorina	2 hours	Celebrated Shona's birthday
18th June	Yoga	Brunswick Community Centre	Ruth, Jackie	1 hours	New instructor this week
20th July	Game Night	Vivian's house	Lisa, Viv, Val, Dionne, RJ	4 hours	Played Trivial Pursuit. Viv won again! (I think she cheats Lol)
22nd Aug	Rummikub afternoon	Park Slope cafe	Michael, Brian, Liza, Sam, Pam	2 hours	Introduced Samuel to the game

Need more pages to create an action plan or log your habits? Scan the QR code below with your smartphone to get access to free extra content to help you improve your habit.
(See page 2 for how to use QR codes)

Scan me

Printables Sheets:

- Social Action Plan
- Social Calendar
- Includes examples

Scan QR code or go to: www.lizalluma.com/after55

Friendship Log Book

Celebrate the moments and connections that bring joy to your life. The Friendship Log Book is a simple, meaningful way to nurture old friendships and build new ones. Capture the special memories, stay connected, and enrich your social life. Scan the QR code or visit **mybook.to/friendship-log-book** to get your copy today!

Scan me

Part Three

Reflection and Action

The journey doesn't end here. Continue refining your lifestyle routine to enhance your overall health and well-being. Regular reflection and self-assessment will help you maintain healthy habits, stay on track, and progressively improve over time.

Remember, each step you take is building towards a healthier, happier you—embrace the journey and see how far you can go!

"YOU DON'T STOP LAUGHING WHEN YOU GROW OLD, YOU GROW OLD WHEN YOU STOP LAUGHING!"

Looking Back to Move Forward

> *Keep looking up...*
> *that's the secret of life.*
> *—Snoopy*

As you move forward, take a moment to reflect on the changes you've started. Have you found joy in increased physical activity, or noticed how better food choices have affected your energy? How about your sleep—has it improved? And don't overlook the importance of feeling more at ease and nurturing stronger friendships.

Improvement in these areas is a gradual process, each step forward a testament to your commitment. It's all about taking it one day at a time, celebrating the small victories, and maintaining a positive outlook.

In the next section, you'll reflect on your progress and plan your next steps. This is your chance to celebrate your achievements and keep building toward a healthier, happier future. Embrace this opportunity to shape your journey ahead.

Reevaluating Your Quality of Life

How do you feel now about your current levels of health and happiness?

How was your journey? Write down your replies to the questions below to find out how you're going in each area of your life. *Remember, don't overthink it—just write.*

1. SLEEP: Are you sleeping better each night? Are there any factors, such as stress or screen time, that may still be affecting your sleep?

2. EXERCISE: Did you increase your physical activity? How have you engaged in regular physical activity?

3. NUTRITION: Did you change your diet? Are you satisfied with your eating habits? If not, why?

4. ALCOHOL: How have you noticed any changes in your drinking habits or the effects of alcohol on your well-being?

5. PHYSICAL HEALTH: Have you been experiencing any symptoms, pain, or changes in energy levels? If so, jot down your thoughts.

6. MENTAL WELL-BEING: Are there any persistent thoughts or emotions that are concerning you, or any positive changes in your mental well-being that you've noticed?

7. FRIENDSHIPS: Reflect on your interactions with friends and family recently. How have your relationships been?

Spinning the Wellness Wheel Again

Complete and compare it to your first Wellness Wheel on page 27.

1) Rate your current level of satisfaction in each lifestyle segment on a scale of 1-10 *(10 being the highest).*

2) Shade in each segment of the wheel according to your satisfaction number.

3) Assess the overall picture, noticing where areas of improvement are needed.

5) Implement changes: Focus on the lifestyle sections that you want to improve on by setting a goal, tracking your habits and reflecting on them.

EXAMPLE

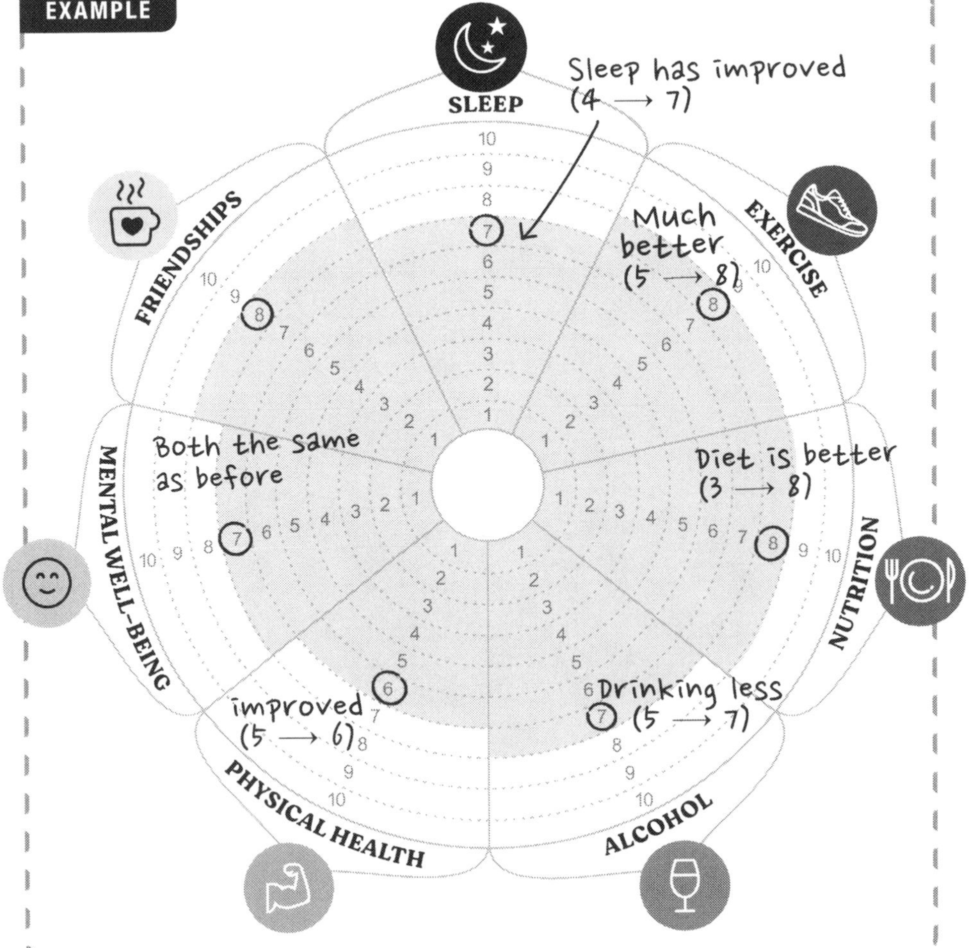

Now, over to you...

Add your notes here:

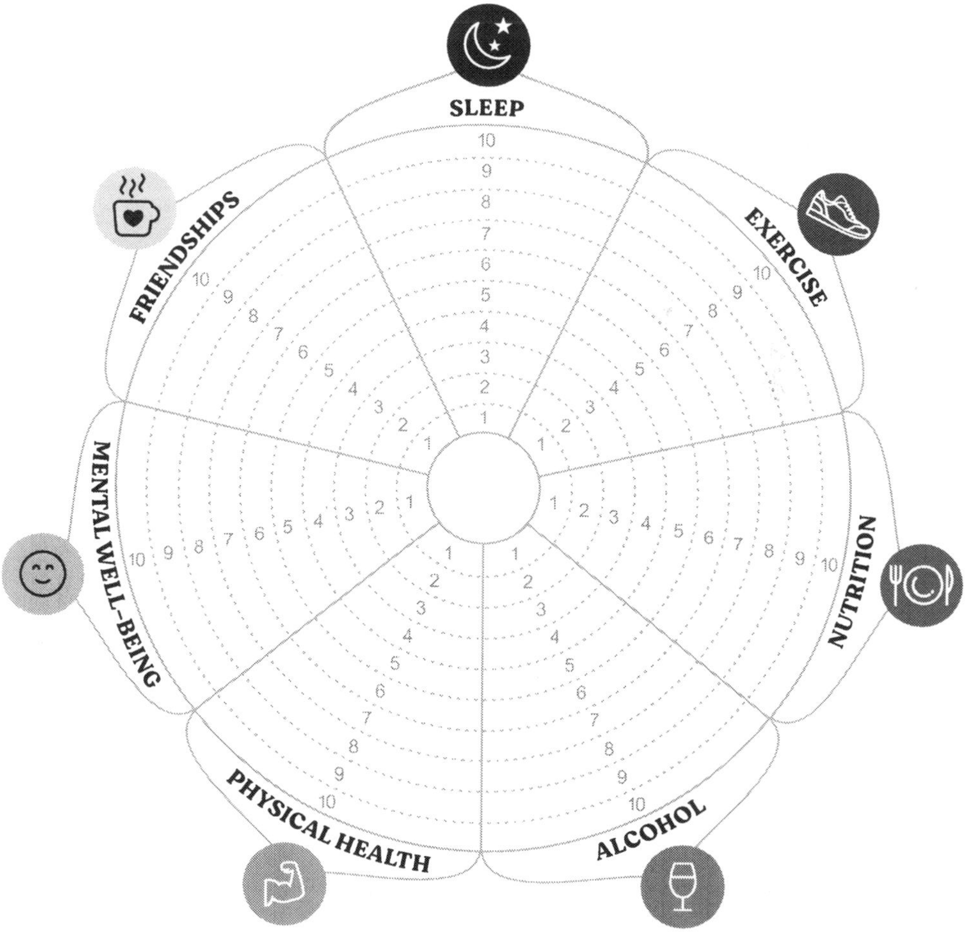

Write about what habits or lifestyle changes you will continue to incorporate into your life:

BUCKET LIST
GET BUCKET
... ?

Bucket List Dreams

Life's milestones don't end at 50; they become the stepping stones to greater adventures. ”

Life's milestones don't end at the halfway mark; they become the stepping stones to greater adventures. You might think that the term "bucket list" is reserved for the younger crowd, but trust me, it's never too late for you to dream big and set exciting goals. Reaching this stage in life is not a finish line; it's the beginning of a new chapter for you, filled with endless opportunities to explore, grow, and savor life's sweet moments.

You've been working hard on your health and well-being, and now's your chance to enjoy the fruits of your labor. So, grab a pen and let's get started on creating a bucket list that'll make your heart race and your spirit soar. After all, your age is just a number, and your adventure has no expiration date!

Create Your Bucket List

	Personal Development	Travel & Adventure	Experiences & Events
***Short-term** (in the next 12 months)*			
EXAMPLE	Take a Italian cooking class	Go on a road trip across the country	Attend a live music concert
***Long-term** (1 ~ 5 years from now)*			
EXAMPLE	Write my autobiography	See the Northern Lights in Finland	Go whale watching

List your short-term goals for the next 12 months as well as your long-term goals for 1 to 5 years from now.

Family & Friendships	Community & Giving Back	Health & Wellness
write down life advice for my family	volunteer for a cause	Add regular physical activity into my routine
organize a big family reunion	contribute to environmental conservation	complete a 3 mile walk or run

From Dreams to Reality: *Step-by-Step*

1) Write down one of your Bucket List items below:

2) When do you want to achieve it by:

3) What are the specific details in achieving it:
(e.g. do you need 'X' dollars or do certain conditions need to be met first? Be as detailed as possible.)

Appendix A

Scan me

Need more pages to create an action plan or log your habits? Scan the QR code below with your smartphone to get access to free extra worksheets to help you improve your habit.
(See page 2 for how to use QR codes)
Website: www.lizalluma.com/after55

Appendix B

Resources and Recommended Reading

I wholeheartedly believe in sharing valuable ideas and work from others, and in that spirit, I share these listings of resources that I've found helpful.

SLEEP
Why We Sleep by Matthew Walker PhD
Sleepy, podcast by Otis Gray to help you snooze (sleepyradio.com)
National Sleep Foundation (thensf.org)

EXERCISE
AllTrails (alltrails.com), database of hiking trails/outdoor activities
SilverSneakers (Youtube Channel), aimed at older adults
Flipping 50 with Debra Atkinson (Youtube Channel), for women
Body Groove (Youtube Channel), fun dance workouts for adults

NUTRITION
Nutrition Facts by Dr. Michael Greger (NutritionFacts.org)
British Nutrition Foundation (BNF), (nutrition.org.uk)
Cooked by Michael Pollan (Netflix documentary series)

ALCOHOL
Moderation Management (moderation.org), support groups and resources
SMART Recovery (smartrecoveryinternational.org), self-help support groups and resources for any addiction

PHYSICAL HEALTH

Harvard School of Public Health (hsph.harvard.edu)
Mayo Clinic (mayoclinic.org)

MENTAL WELL-BEING

The Happiness Lab with Dr. Laurie Santos, a feel-good podcast
Mindful (mindful.org), articles, guided meditations, and resources for incorporating mindfulness and meditation into your daily life
Craftsy (craftsy.com), online classes in various crafts like knitting, sewing, quilting, painting, and more
The Nature Conservancy (nature.org), volunteer opportunities for conservation efforts like tree planting, trail maintenance, wildlife monitoring, and connecting people with nature

FRIENDSHIPS

Meetup (meetup.com), connects people through local events, fostering shared interests like outdoor activities and volunteering
VolunteerMatch (volunteermatch.org), connects people with local volunteer opportunities based on interests, fostering community connections and giving back

HEALTHY AGING

Age Proof by Professor Rose Anne Kenny
How Not to Age by Dr. Michael Greger

HABITS & INSPIRATION

The Happiness Advantage by Shawn Achor
Atomic Habits by James Clear
The Moth, podcast that features true stories told live by people from various backgrounds and walks of life

Emergency Information

PERSONAL DETAILS	
Name:	Phone:
Address:	

In case of an emergency please contact:	
Name:	Phone:
Relationship:	Email:
Name:	Phone:
Relationship:	Email:

MEDICAL HISTORY	
Blood type: *(A+, A-, B+, B-, AB+, AB-, O+, O-)*	
Previous surgeries and medical events:	
Medications and supplements you are taking:	

MEDICAL HISTORY	
Chronic diseases: *(such as diabetes, hypertension, asthma, etc.)*	
Heart conditions: *(such as angina, heart attack, heart failure, etc.)*	
Allergies: *(such as food allergies, medication allergies, insect bite/ sting allergies, etc.)*	
Respiratory conditions: *(such as emphysema, chronic bronchitis, etc.)*	
Neurological conditions: *(such as epilepsy, migraines, etc.)*	
Mental well-being conditions: *(such as depression, anxiety, bipolar disorder, etc.)*	
Other	

Please review this book

If you've enjoyed this book and found the insights valuable, please consider leaving a review on the platform where you purchased it. Your feedback not only supports me as an author but also helps other readers discover and benefit from these teachings. Positive reviews greatly improve the book's visibility and help others find the guidance they might be seeking. Remember, sharing your thoughts contributes to the community and spreads a little good karma. I appreciate your time and thank you for helping to spread wellness and positivity!

With gratitude,

Liza Lluma

About the Author

Liza Lluma is an Australian graphic designer and mum who ran away to live in a small medieval town near the Pre-Pyrenees mountains in Catalonia, Spain. In her quest for simplicity, she often finds herself complicating life, whether by delving into the pH levels of her backyard dirt or nurturing her modest veggie patch, which provides a welcome retreat from the digital world. A fervent advocate of whole-food, plant-based diets, Liza preaches the vibrant flavors of whole foods to anyone who will listen. She also extols the virtues of getting your hands dirty, both literally in her garden and metaphorically in life.

Her latest book, *How To Thrive After 55*, breaks down healthy aging into easy, practical steps. Designed to be straightforward and engaging, it shows readers that maintaining health as they age can be simple and enjoyable.

When not tethered to her computer or lost in her garden, Liza crafts illustrations that capture the humor and beauty of everyday life. She is dedicated to empowering others to shape their own destinies and embrace vibrant, fulfilling lives, approaching aging with confidence and style. For Liza, aging isn't about slowing down; it's about taking control to infuse every day with vitality, laughter, and perhaps a bit of good bacteria.

www.instagram.com/liza_lluma

www.facebook.com/lizalluma

www.lizalluma.com/after55

hello@lizalluma.com

Thrive After 55 Habit Tracker Series

Complete your journey to wellness: Get all 7 log books and the main guidebook on Amazon or at **www.lizalluma.com/after55**

Made in the USA
Columbia, SC
27 November 2024

47785843R00113